from COLORING THE SIGNS
LOVED ONES IN SPIRIT

An Adult Coloring Book to Help
Identify Signs from the Other Side

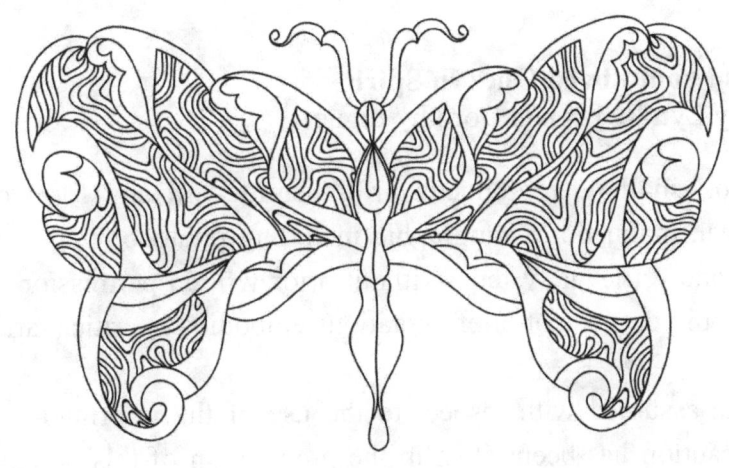

by Authors
Lyn Ragan and Dorothy Pigue

To all of our Loved Ones in Heaven,
With Unconditional Love
and Beautiful Grace...

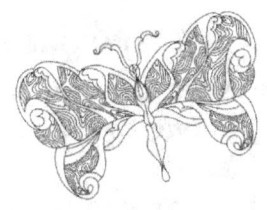

Other Books by Lyn Ragan & Dorothy Pigue

Shading The Colors of Grief and Healing
An Adult Coloring Book To Help Heal Through Grief
fb/shadingthecolorsoflife

Coloring The Shades of Grief and Healing
A Teen/Young Adult Coloring Book To Help Heal Through Grief
fb/shadingthecolorsoflife

Shading Spiritual Signs & Symbols
An Adult Coloring Book
fb/shadingthecolorsoflife

Shading The Power Of The Mandala
An Adult Coloring Book
fb/shadingthecolorsoflife

Shading The Colors Of The Feminine Zodiac
An Adult Coloring Book
fb/shadingthecolorsoflife

Other Books by Lyn Ragan

Wake Me Up! a true story
How Chip's Afterlife Saved Me

We Need To Talk
Living With The Afterlife

Signs From The Afterlife
Identifying Gifts From The Other Side

Signs From Pets In The Afterlife
Identifying Messages From Pets In Heaven

Introduction

Lyn Ragan lost the *love of her life* in 2008. One second they were chatting on the phone and in the next, he was killed while preparing for work.

Her grief spiraled into a web of sadness she found difficult to break free of. All of their future dreams destroyed and her life altered forever, Lyn was taken by surprise when she started receiving communications from her deceased fiancé— via dreams. Ms. Ragan would later write about their visits and eventually publish several books on the subject of *Afterlife Communications*.

Her mission in life is to help those who grieve from the loss of a loved one; her ultimate goal to replace painful grief with belief and understanding. Lyn works tirelessly helping those she can reach to understand this physical life is not the end of who we are, and that love and life lives forever— as do our Souls.

Dorothy Pigue was born into a family of clairvoyants. As a young child, she began hearing the voices of spirits around her. It took many years for Dorothy to realize she could communicate with the spirit world and with loved ones who have crossed over. Wanting to enhance her gifts and psychic abilities, she trained with Carl Woodall at the *Atlanta Metaphysical Center* in Atlanta, Georgia, and became a graduate of *The Anastasi System of Psychic Development* in 2014.

Dorothy is also a Master Herbalist who has been practicing as a Korean Medicine Woman since 1996. She is a Clinical Certified Hypnotherapist, a Certified Usui/Holy Fire Reiki ® Practitioner, and an author.

Dorothy's mission in life is to share her gifts and abilities in hopes of removing the *pain of grief*. Healing begins with love and from the other side, *Love* is the message she enjoys sharing.

Authors Lyn Ragan and Dorothy Pigue are excited to come together on a personal undertaking to help bring peace, love, and healing into the hearts of those who grieve.

Our Wish For You...

*S*igns from your loved ones are delivered everyday, but some messages are given in ways that require more interpretation and extra awareness. From the other side, loved ones use signs and symbols to connect with family and friends left behind on this earthly plane. Oftentimes, the gifts they share are difficult to identify.

Mastering a new language is hard work, but learning to speak the *Language of Spirit* is even more difficult. This coloring book can help you in identifying your signs, your messages, and your symbols from your special one(s) in Heaven.

Our wish is to help you cope with your loss, witness your special sign, and receive *healing* at the same time. That is why we produced this coloring book. Each illustration on the following pages is associated with thousands of documented communications from around the world.

From our personal experiences, we believe each one of these signs is a dynamic blueprint of acceptance, healing, and witnessing messages from our deceased loved ones. Signs from our dear ones are normally very gentle. By their given nature, they do not demand a response nor do they direct you to take an action. Through their appearance however, you are given a spiritual reveal or what we like to describe as— *A BIG HUG FROM HEAVEN*.

Our hope is that these coloring pages will not only help to heal your broken spirit, but also help you in identifying the continued love you receive from your loved one in Heaven. Remember— there is no time limit for your grief and there are no rule books either. Take all the time you need.

One step, one day, and one coloring page... at a time.

Remember— love lives forever, and so do our SOULS.

Dream Visitation

A form of Afterlife connections
between us and them,
our pets,
spirit guides,
and/or angels,
dreams are used to communicate
messages of love and devotion.

Dream-visitations overflow
with peace and love.
Our special ones on the other side
only want for one thing...
to let us know their love
is unconditional.

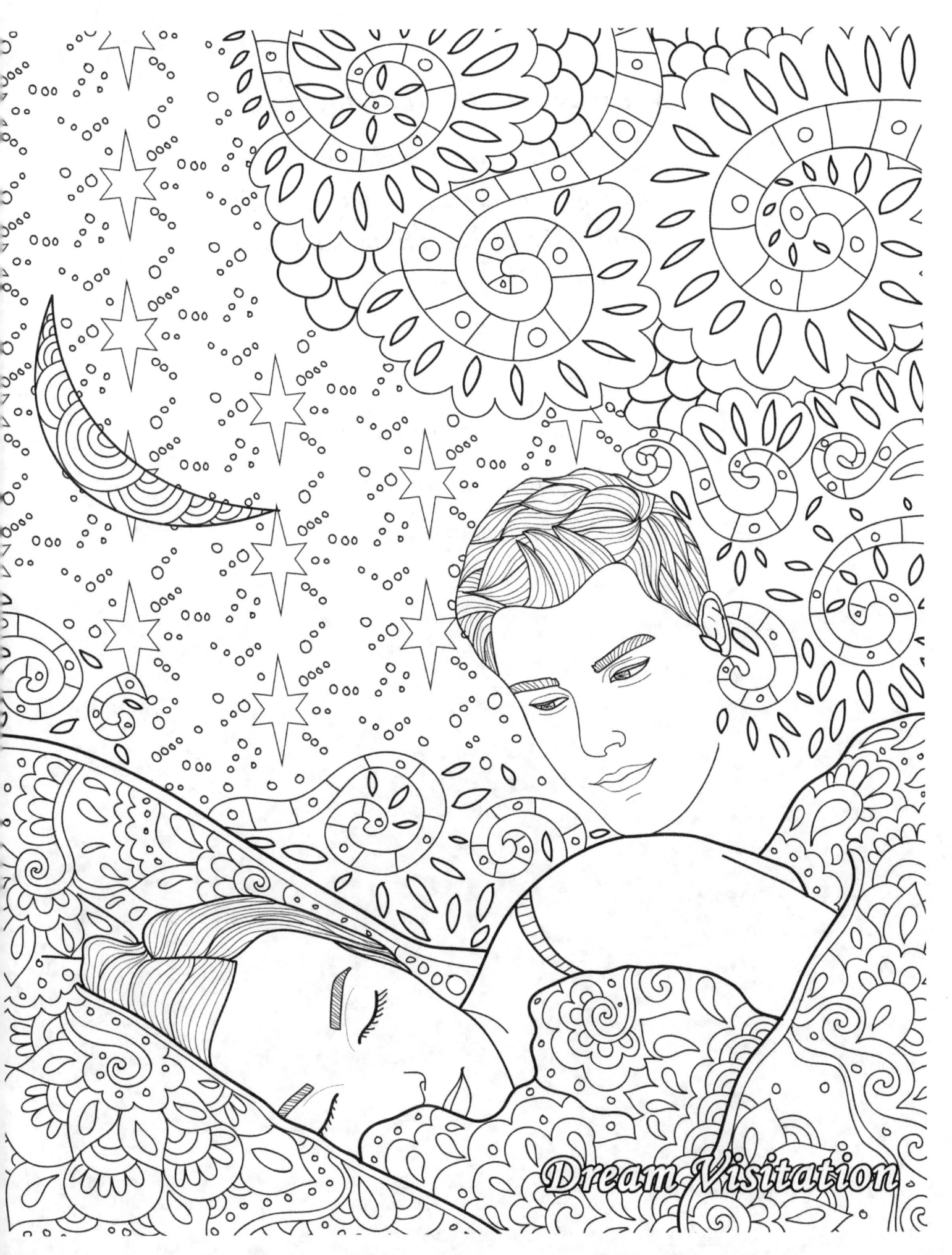

Dream Visitation

Music Is A Universal Language

Songs, music, and lyrics
are huge messages from the Afterlife.
Within the words of a special song,
the love from a dear one
is incredibly palpable.

Music from the other side

is like receiving a kiss

from your loved one

in the Afterlife.

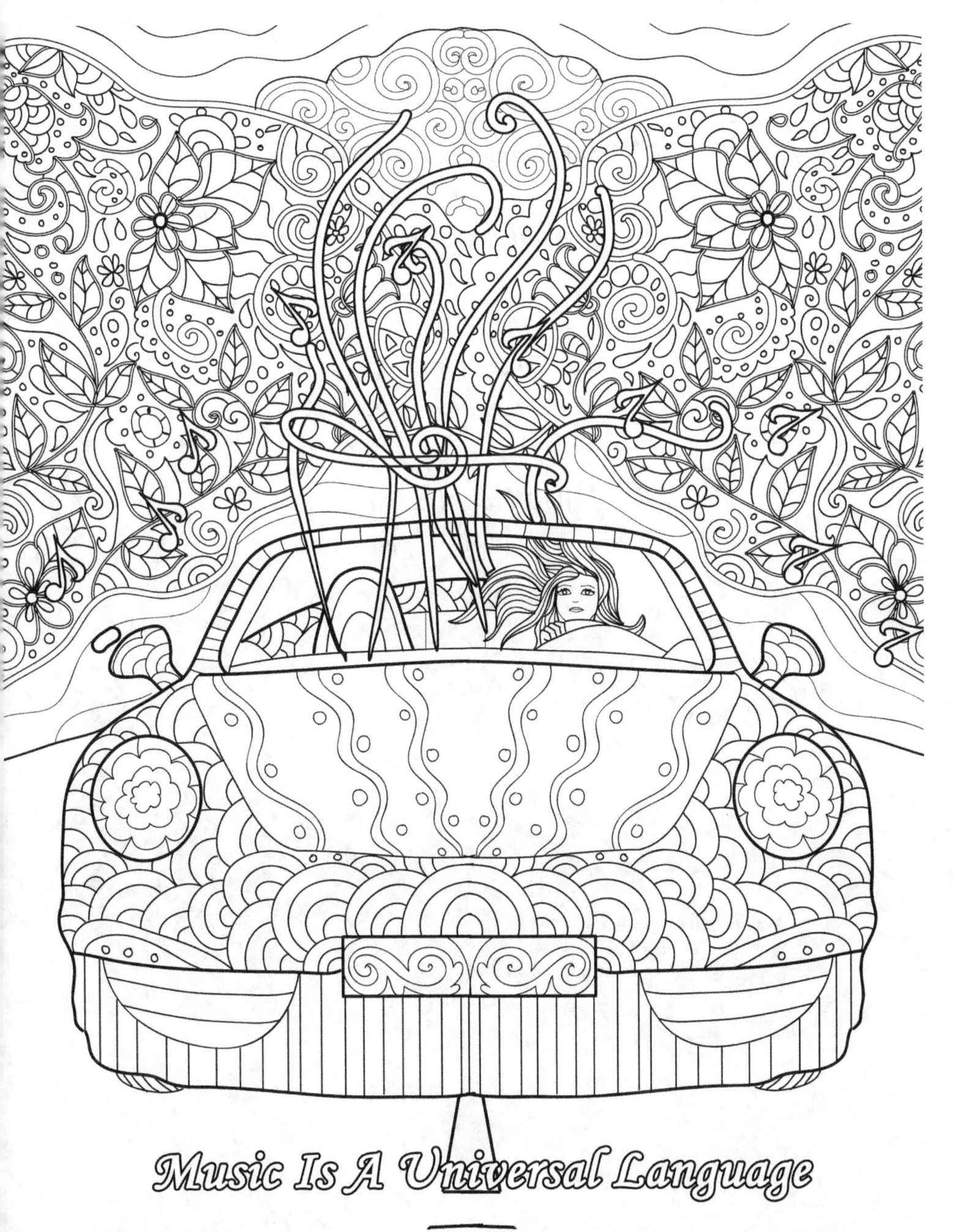

Music Is A Universal Language

Feathers

Symbolizing spiritual evolution
to the higher planes,
feathers often deliver
peace,
joy,
and the feeling of lightness.
They can be a direct link
to the realms of the Afterlife.

When angels are near,
feathers appear.

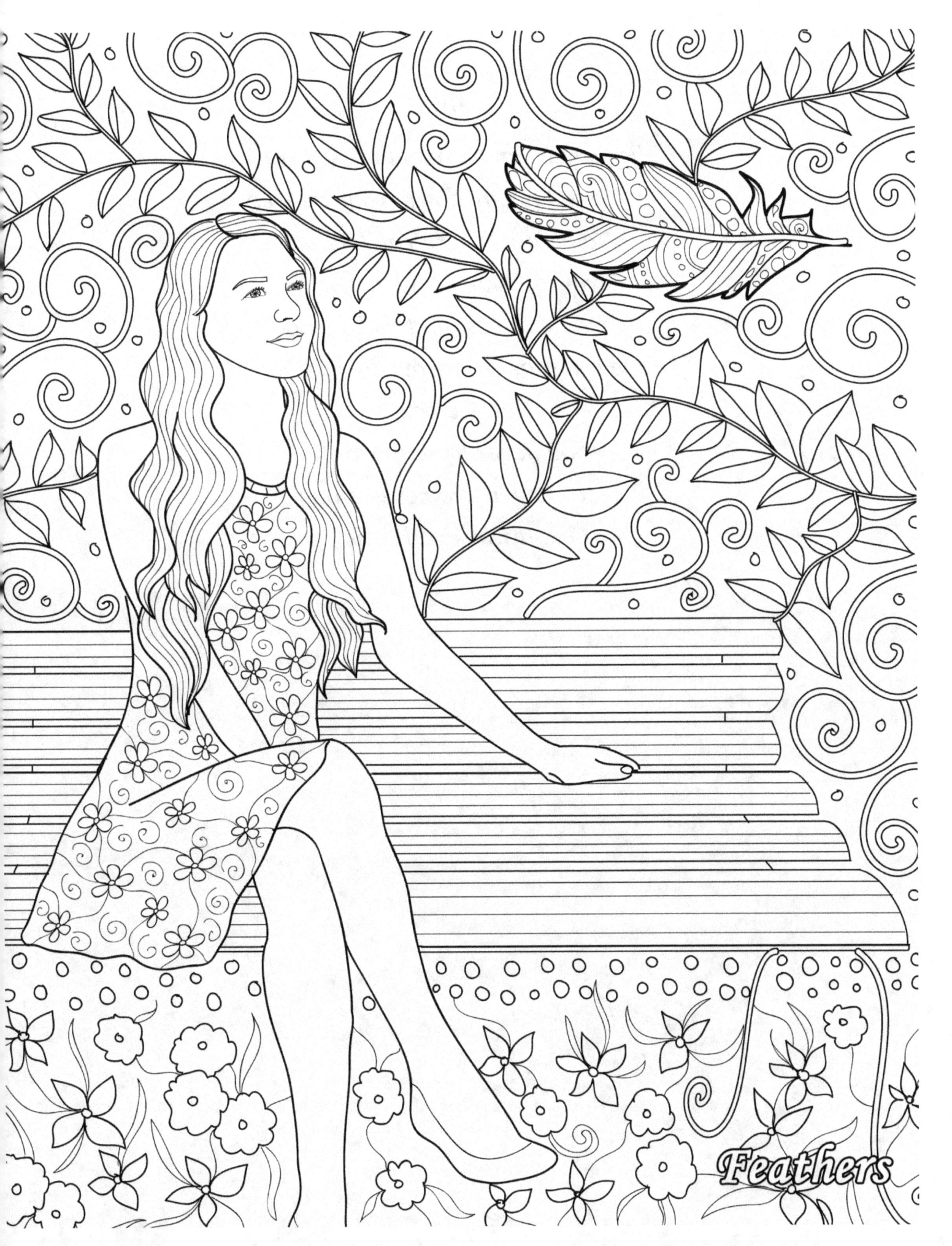

Feathers

Coins

They say when an angel misses you,
they toss a penny down from Heaven.
No matter where you locate
your penny from heaven,
(quarters, dimes, and nickels, too)
the message from your loved one
is very clear...
"You never have to worry
because you are never alone.
I am always with you."

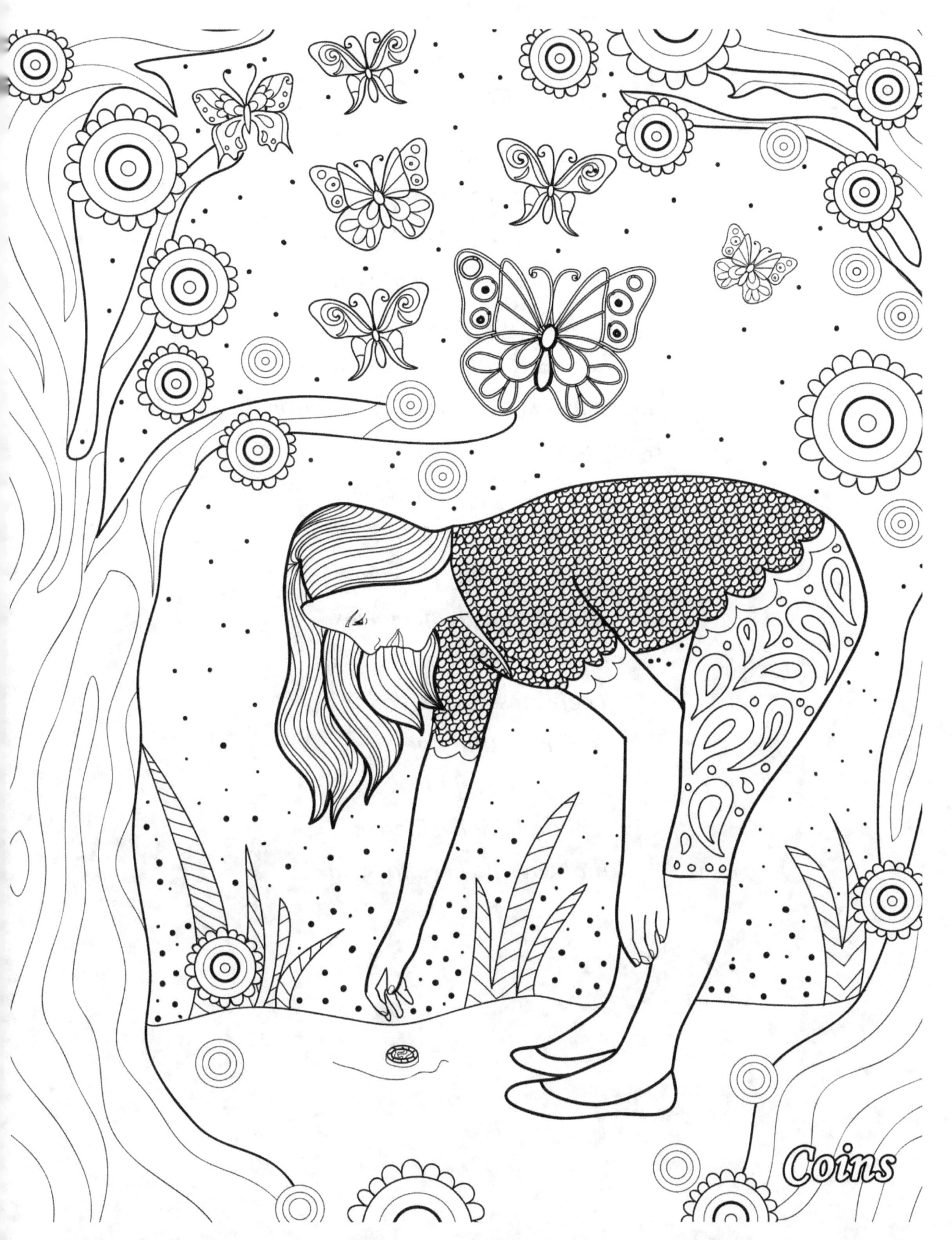

Coins

Flowers

By releasing their
fragrant message,
loved ones teach us
how close they really are.
We are not alone.
There is no other direct sign
that shares such a close connection.
When a loved one sends a message
by way of a specific flower or
a flower's scent,
their desire is to trigger
those special memories
of key moments in our lives.
Their message to you is a
beautiful one...
"I'm right here.
Right here beside you.
I'll always be here for you."

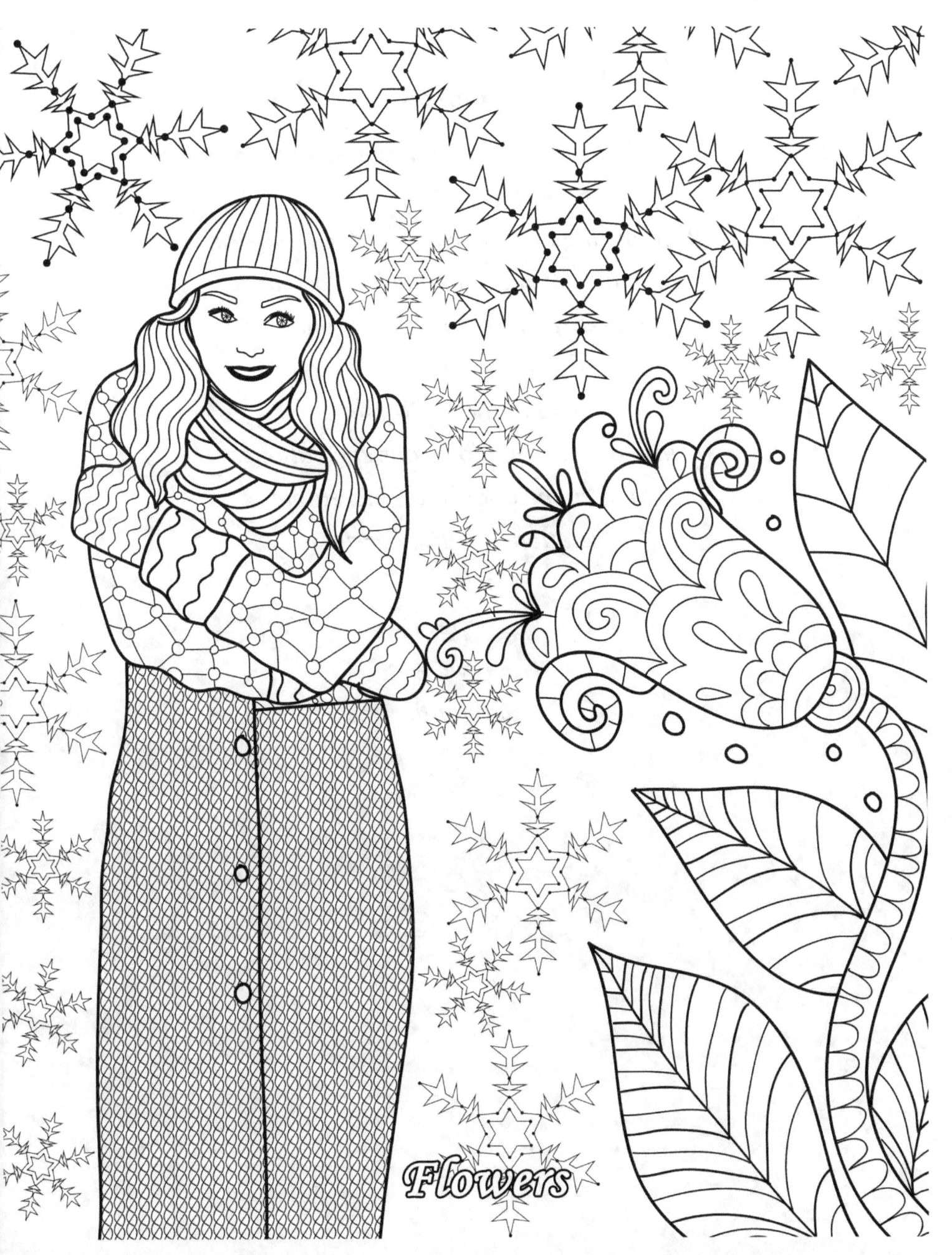

Flowers

Numbers

Numbers are big in the Afterlife.

Really big.

Recognizing and interpreting the numbers

along our journey can help us feel more

closely connected to loved ones,

to our angels,

and to the Universe.

This connection allows our special ones

to open the door to an incredible

relationship that carries

peace,

hope,

love,

and faith.

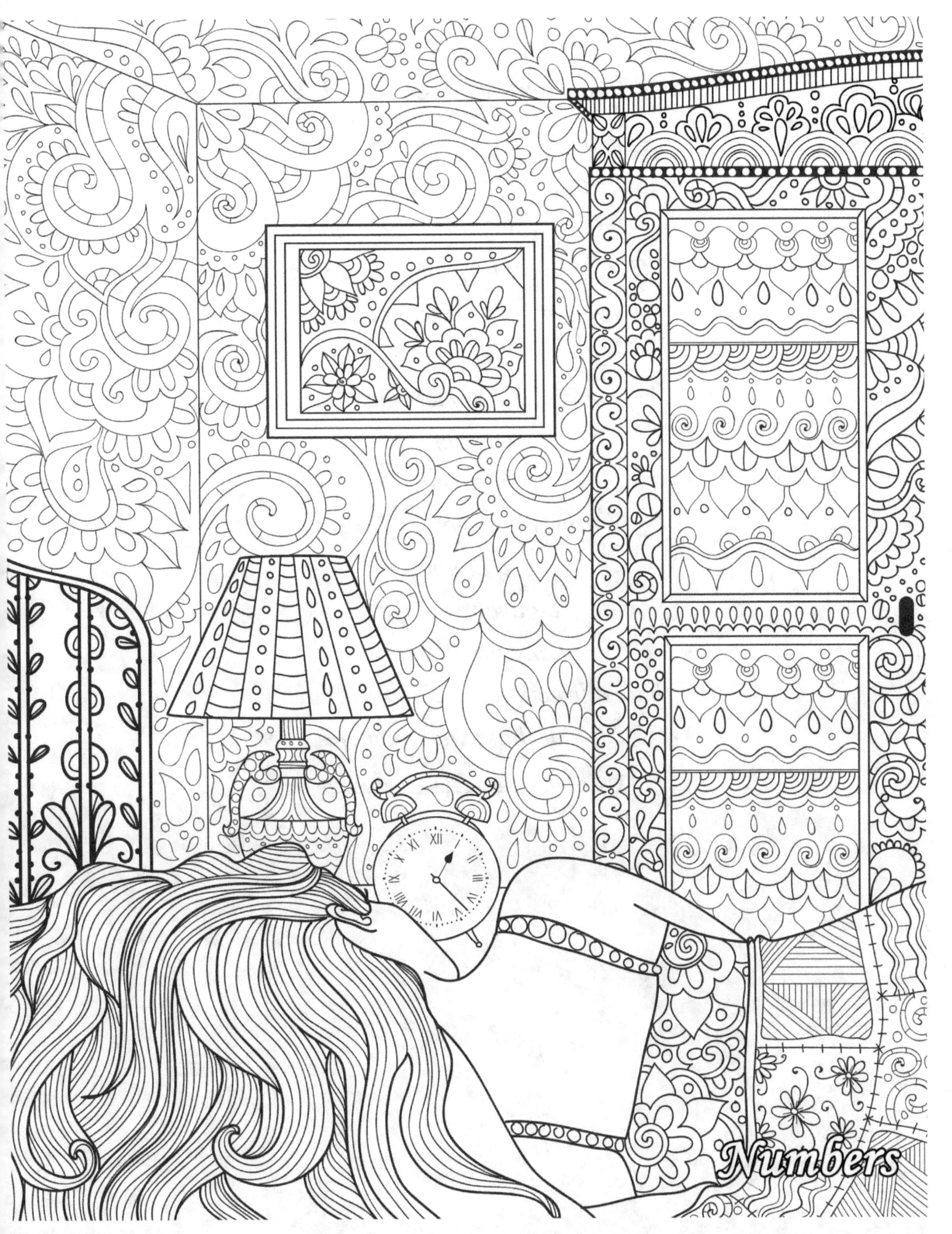

Numbers

The Scent of a Loved One

Scents and smells are a very common
way that our beloved dear ones
let us know they are around.
They give off fragrances we know
we can't question because
we've smelled it before.
When we smell their
perfume,
cologne,
a flower's sweet fragrance,
a cigar,
cigarette smoke,
or any familiar scent
that is directly connected with them,
it's at that exact moment
<u>we know they are beside us</u>.

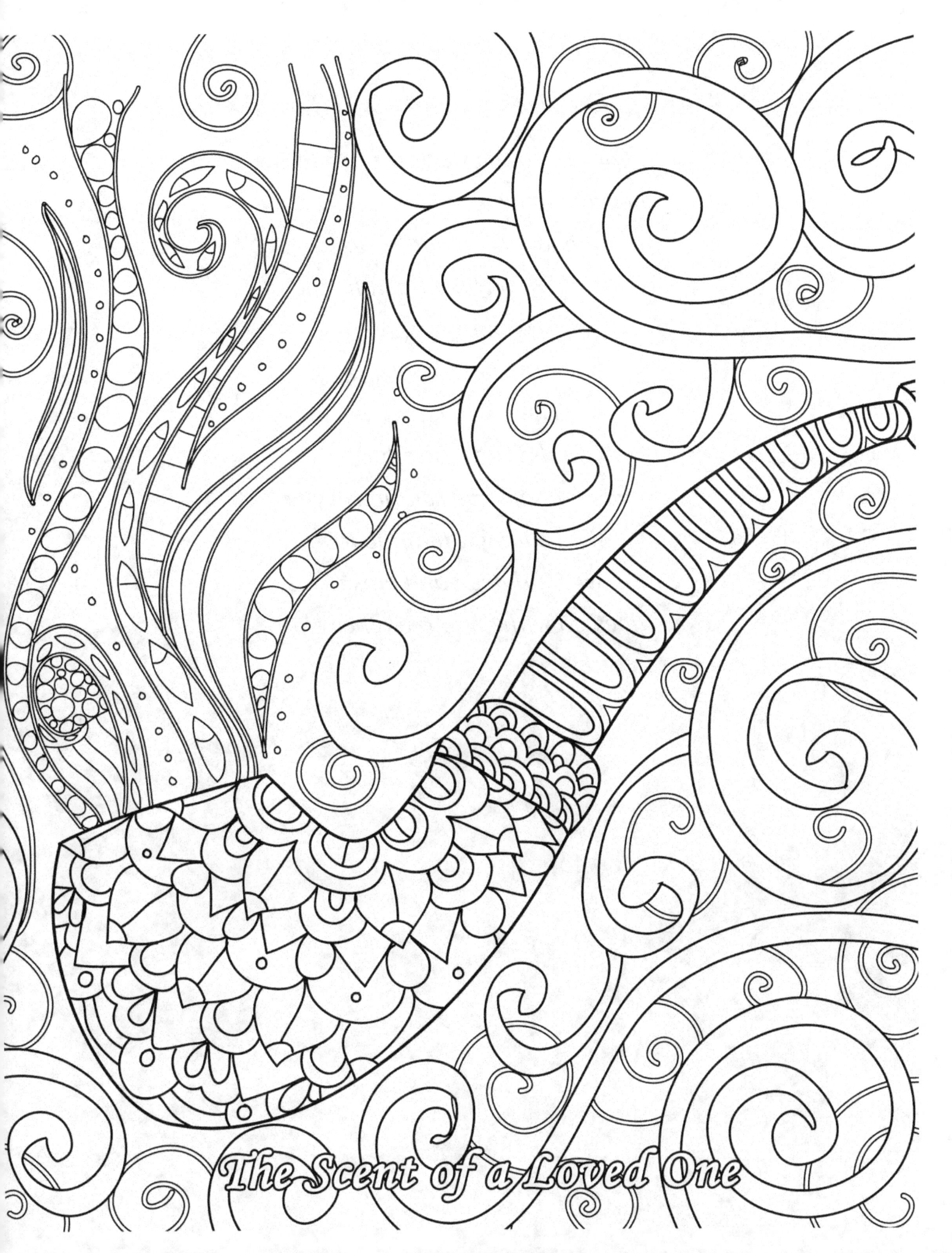

The Scent of a Loved One

Sensing The Presence of Your Loved One

Our loved ones allow us to feel

their presence in order to teach us,

and validate it for us,

that physical death

is not the end

of who we are.

They also teach us

that it is possible

to continue our relationships.

We're taught that the love

we hold dear and close…

does go with us to the other side.

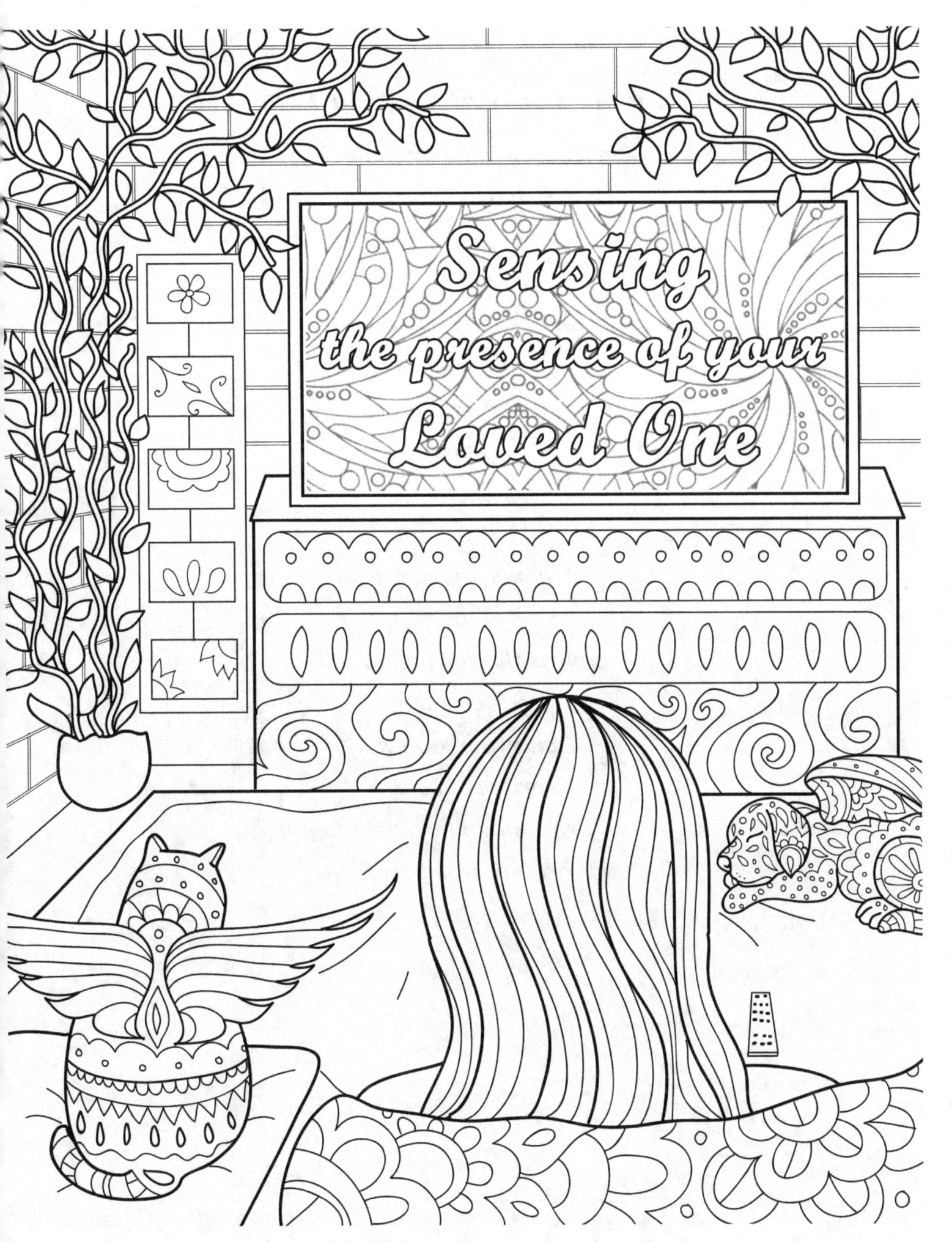

Stones/Rocks Along Your Path

When signs come into our lives,

they have a beautiful

message to share.

It's a very personal

and usually profound

announcement

and one where your

symbol

is a message

of an amazing

communication

of love.

Love is the key ingredient

to everything

and your stones,

or your rocks,

are a magnificent sign

to represent your loved one.

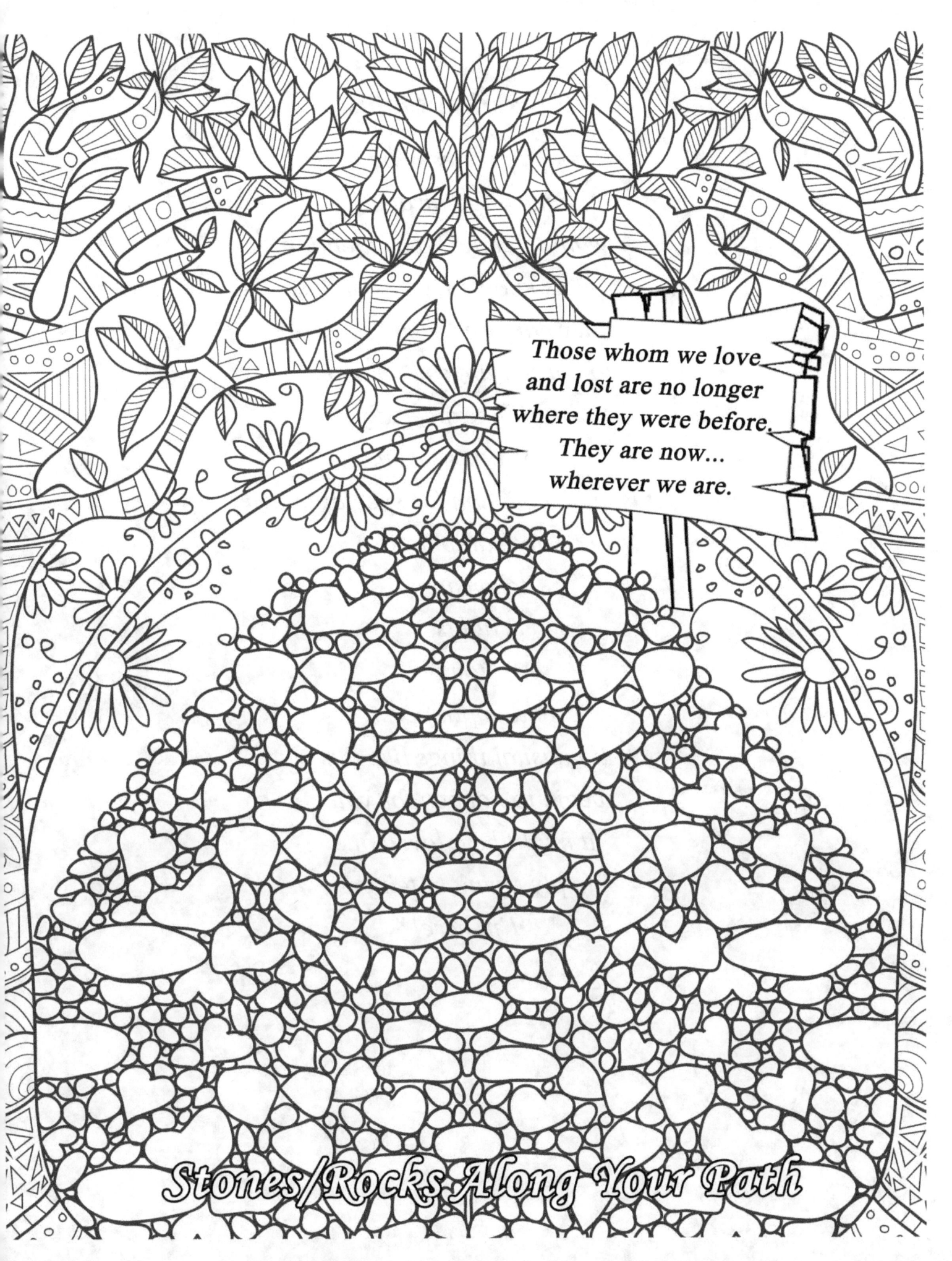

Those whom we love
and lost are no longer
where they were before.
They are now...
wherever we are.

Stones/Rocks Along Your Path

Flickering Lights

When loved ones want to get

a message through,

or want to collect our attention

to let us know they're with us,

they can use their energy

to cause things to snap on

or off unexpectedly.

For this reason,

it is quite common for special ones

to manipulate

televisions,

lights,

toys,

and appliances.

If unusual things like this

begin to happen for you,

it might be a loved one

simply trying to tell you,

"I'm here!"

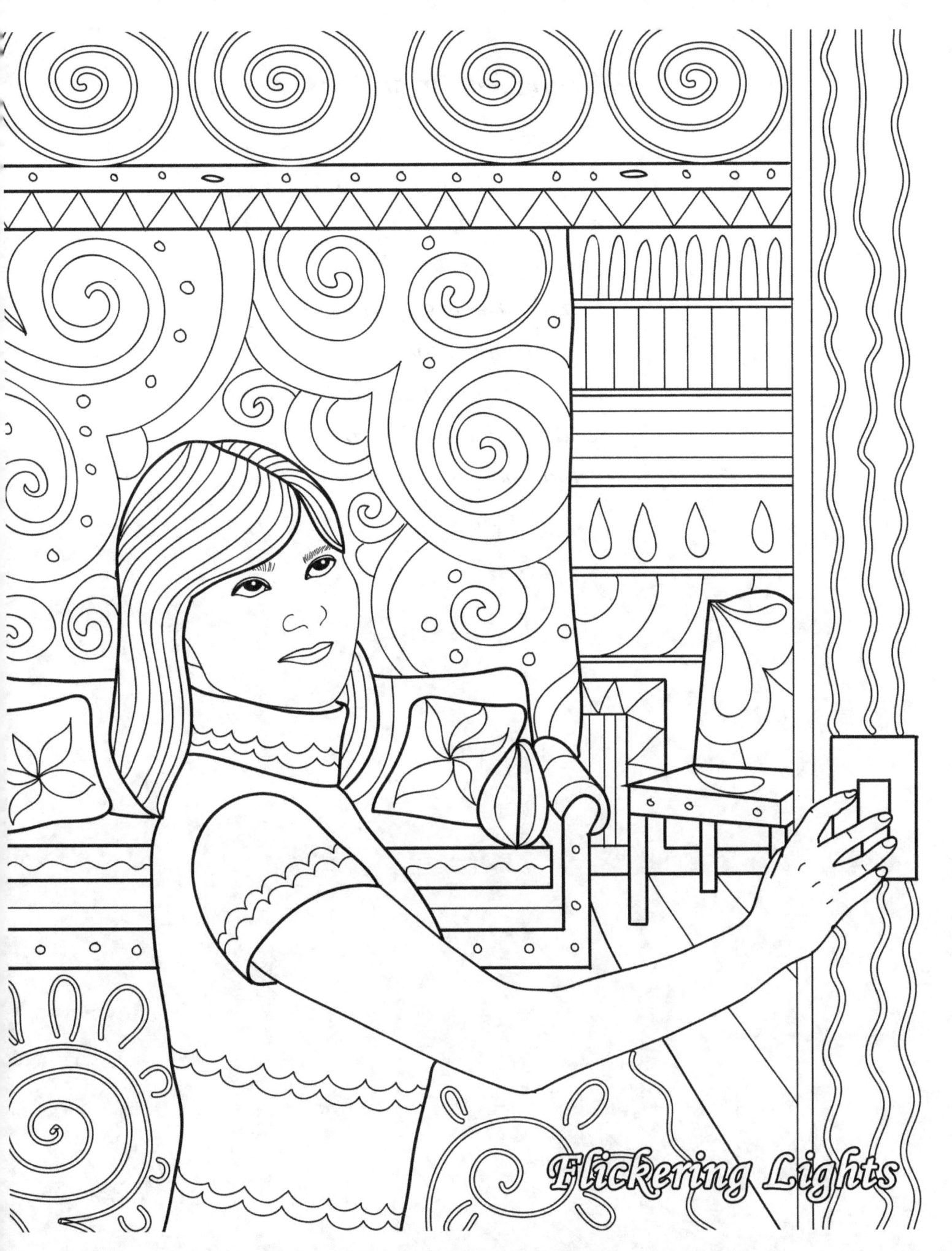

Flickering Lights

Seeing An Apparition

There's more to life
than what can be seen
with the naked eye.
Seeing your loved one
in their energy form
(apparition)
can bring great comfort
and physical validation
that they are always
with you.

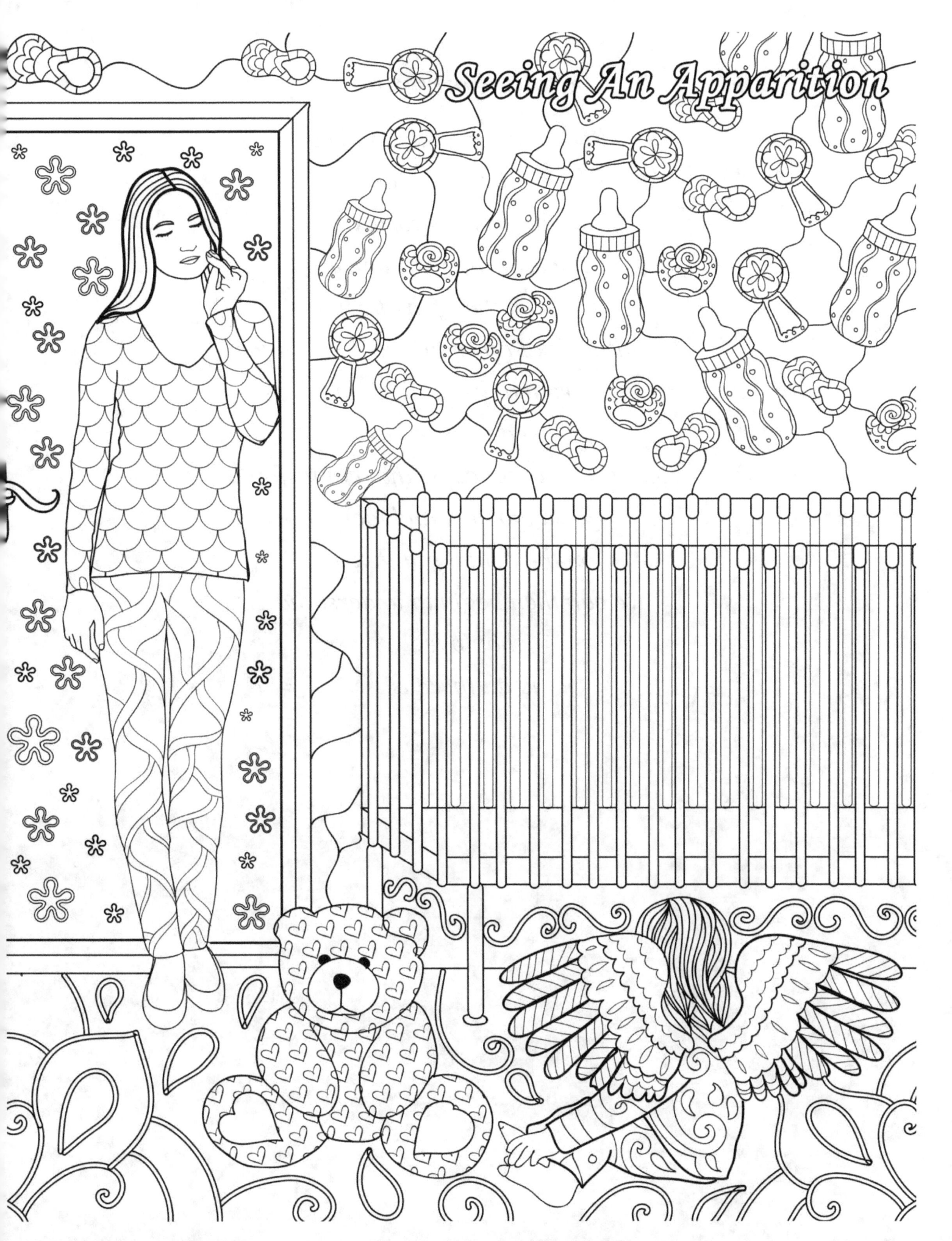

Cloud Formations

Recognizing cloud images
brings about an
awareness of positive
life affirming guidance
from the Afterlife.
It's difficult at times to wrap our minds
around the abilities of
our loved ones in Heaven,
but if we can set aside that confusion
for a moment and focus
on the actual gift given,
we can then begin to understand
*that **love**...*
is all there is.

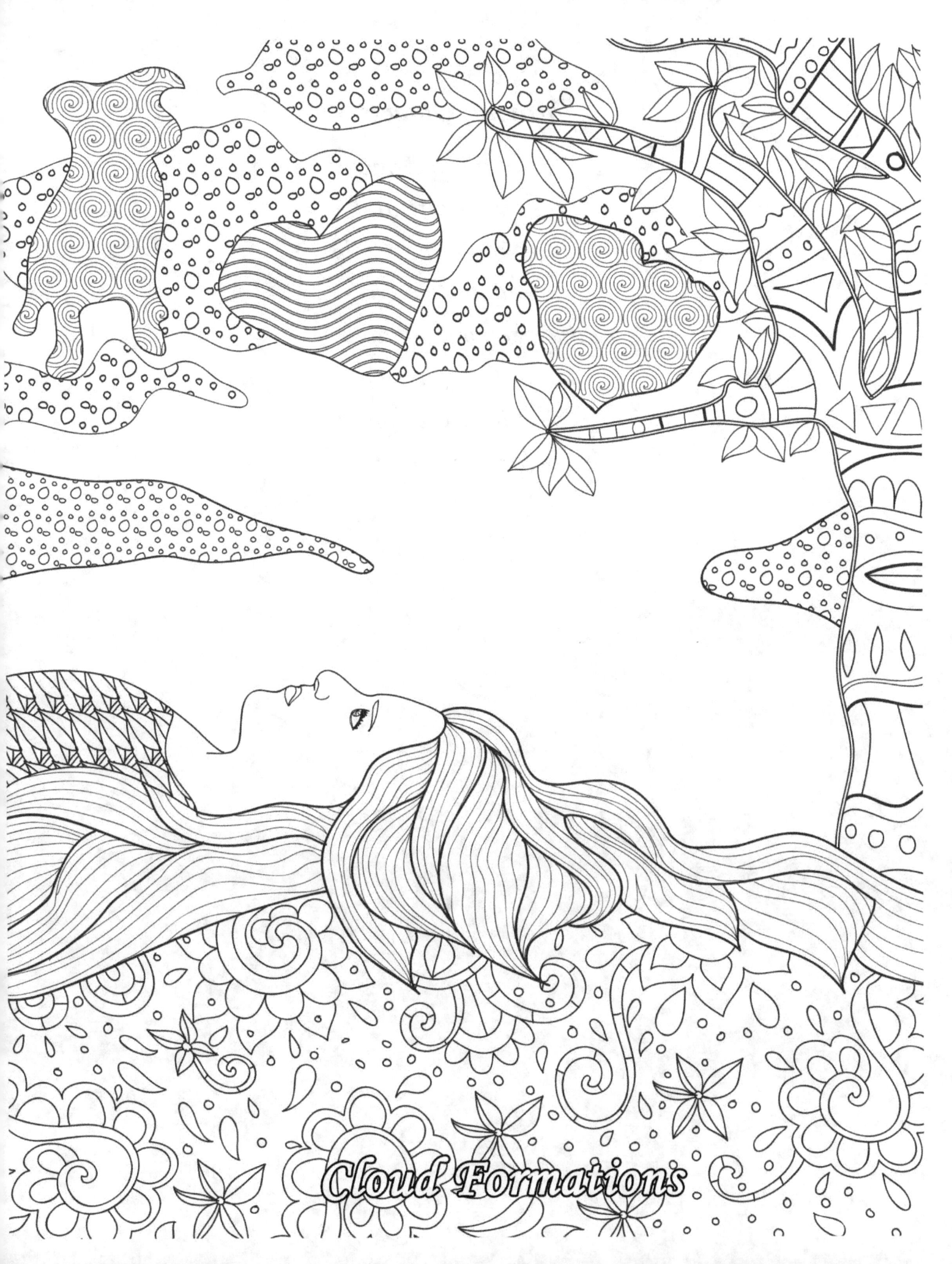

Cloud Formations

Moving Objects

When a loved one
wants your attention,
they go to great lengths
to master
their communication.
Even if they have to
repeat it several times
before you get it.

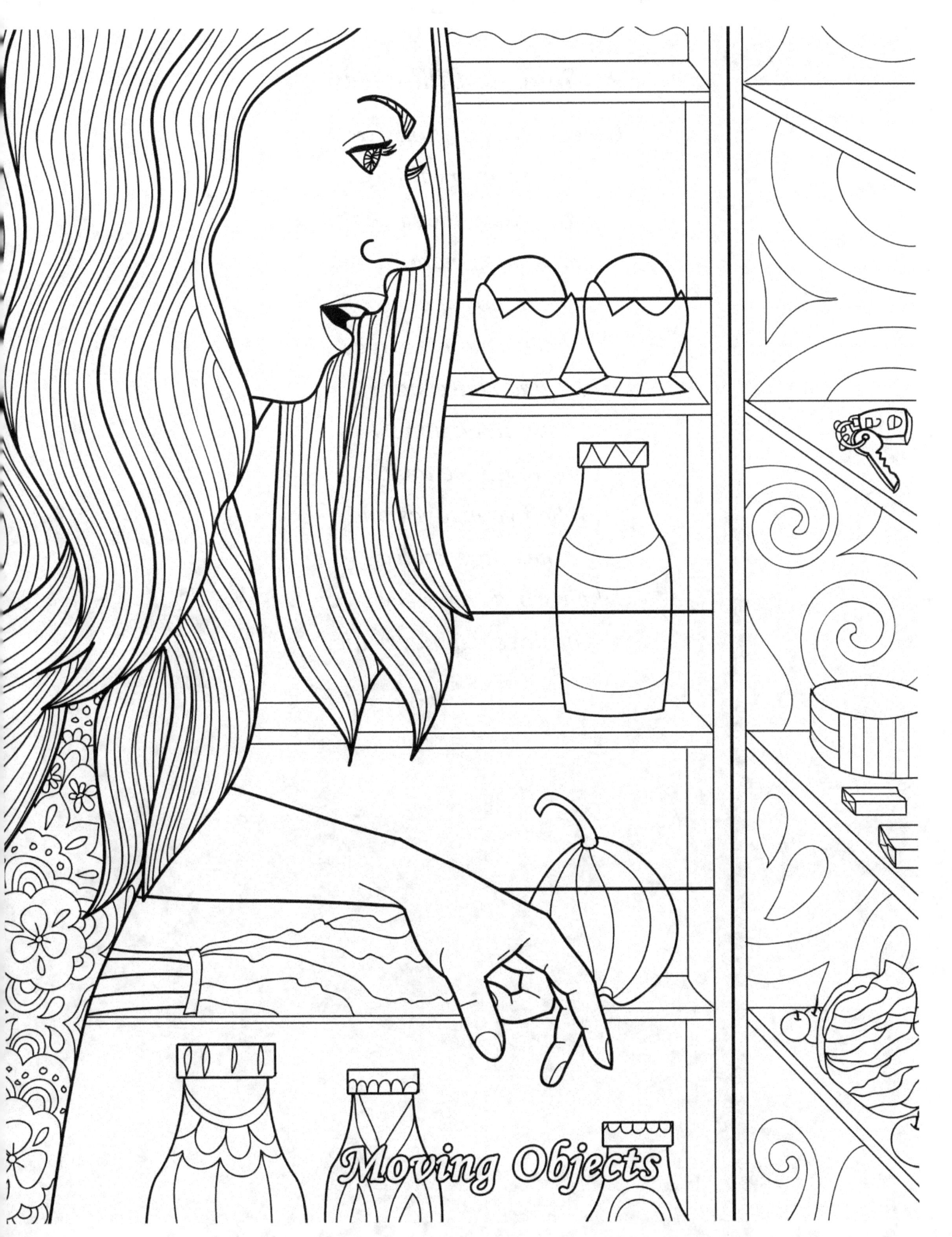

Moving Objects

Signs & Billboards

Loved ones position everyone
and every thing
exactly where they need to be
by using synchronicity
as a tool of choice.
They send messages
and share signs
with the utmost
of divine love.
When your loves one's
message speaks,
their words are very clear,
"Our love can never die."

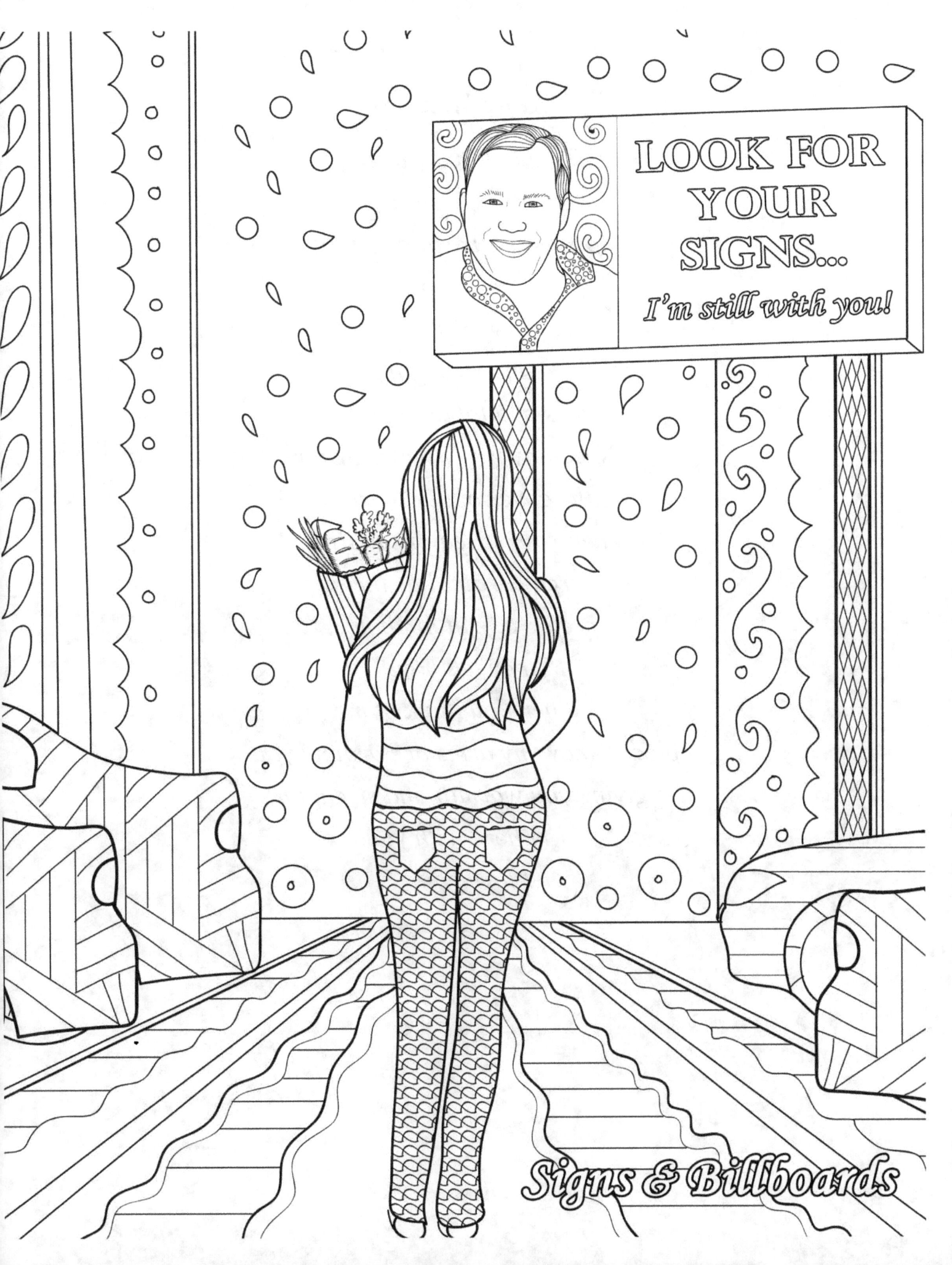

Red Cardinal

Using the Red Cardinal
as their sign,
loved ones remind us that
passion,
warmth,
and strength
is available to us.
Especially while we're under
the cover of dark grief.
When your loved one delivers
a red cardinal as their
preferred gift of choice,
they tell you,
"When you think of me,
please know my arms are around you,
giving you warmth and strength.
I'm here with you.
I love you."

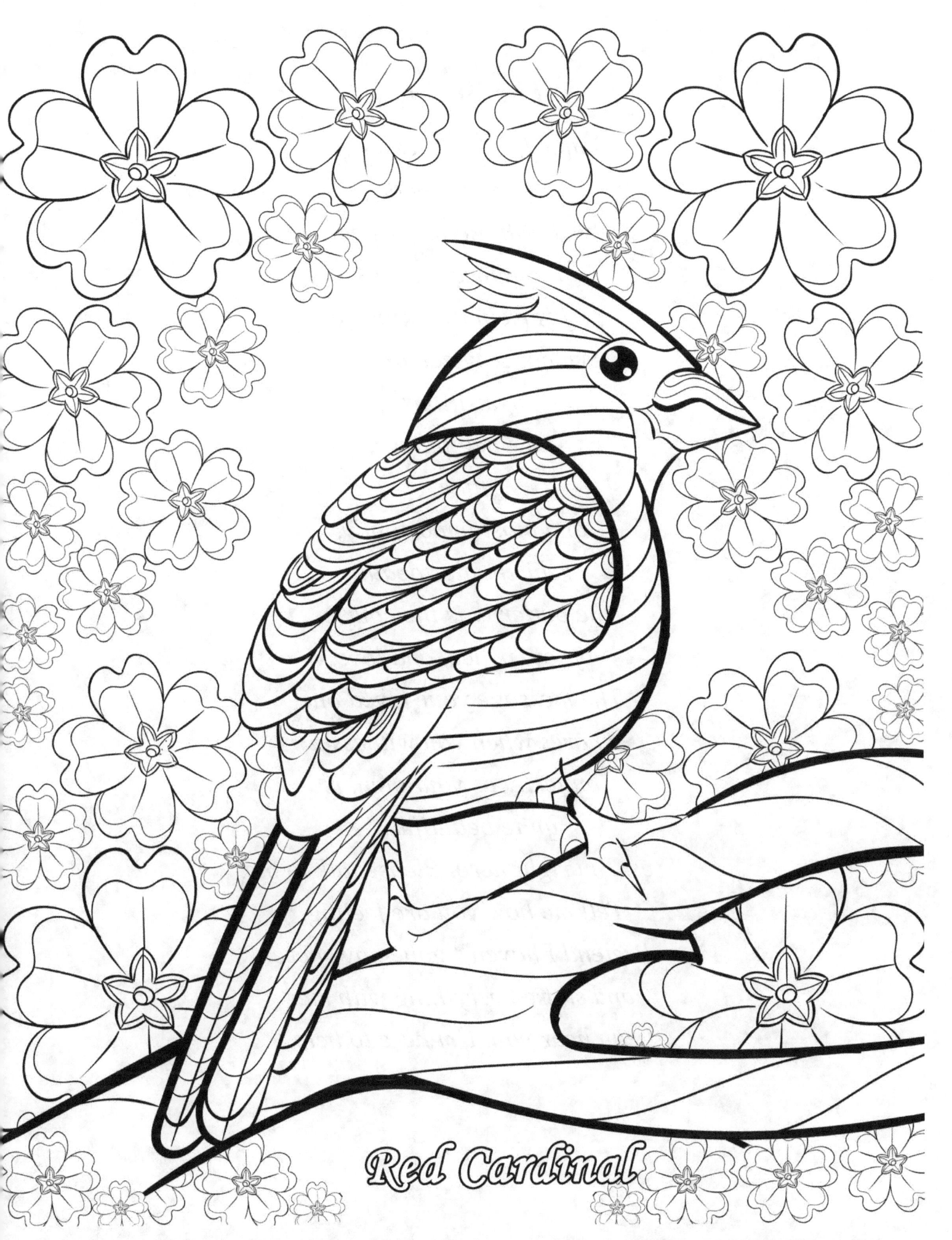

Red Cardinal

The Butterfly

Butterflies are messengers
of the moment.
This is why so many people
recognize them as
signs from the Afterlife.
Symbolizing celebration,
transitions,
new beginnings,
time,
and most importantly,
rebirth after death;
the butterfly is the courier
of joy, peace, and love.
The message your loved one
shares when you witness a
butterfly as your sign, is
quite beautiful…
"Yes, I'm right here. Please talk to me.
Tell me how you are feeling.
Pretend I haven't gone anywhere
and share everything with me.
I can hear you. I'm here to help."

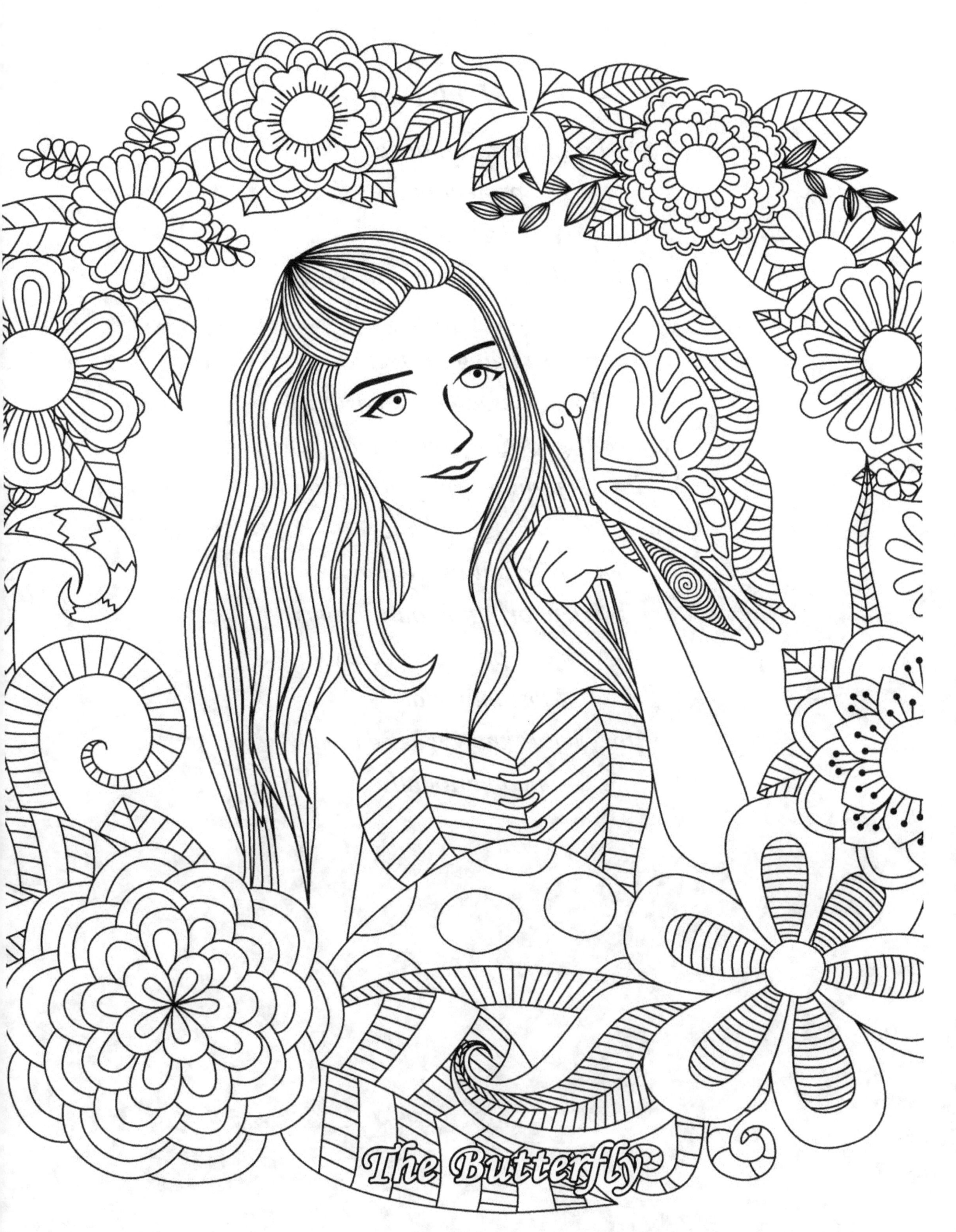

The Butterfly

The LadyBug

Ladybugs symbolize love,

protection,

and good luck.

When the beetles appear in our lives,

loved ones inform us that

we're being protected.

Their message is clear…

"I am your guardian angel and protector.

My love is tightly wrapped around you,

keeping you safe."

They also tell us we can now

work at bringing our dreams

into our physical reality.

Most importantly,

they let us know we are loved,

unconditionally.

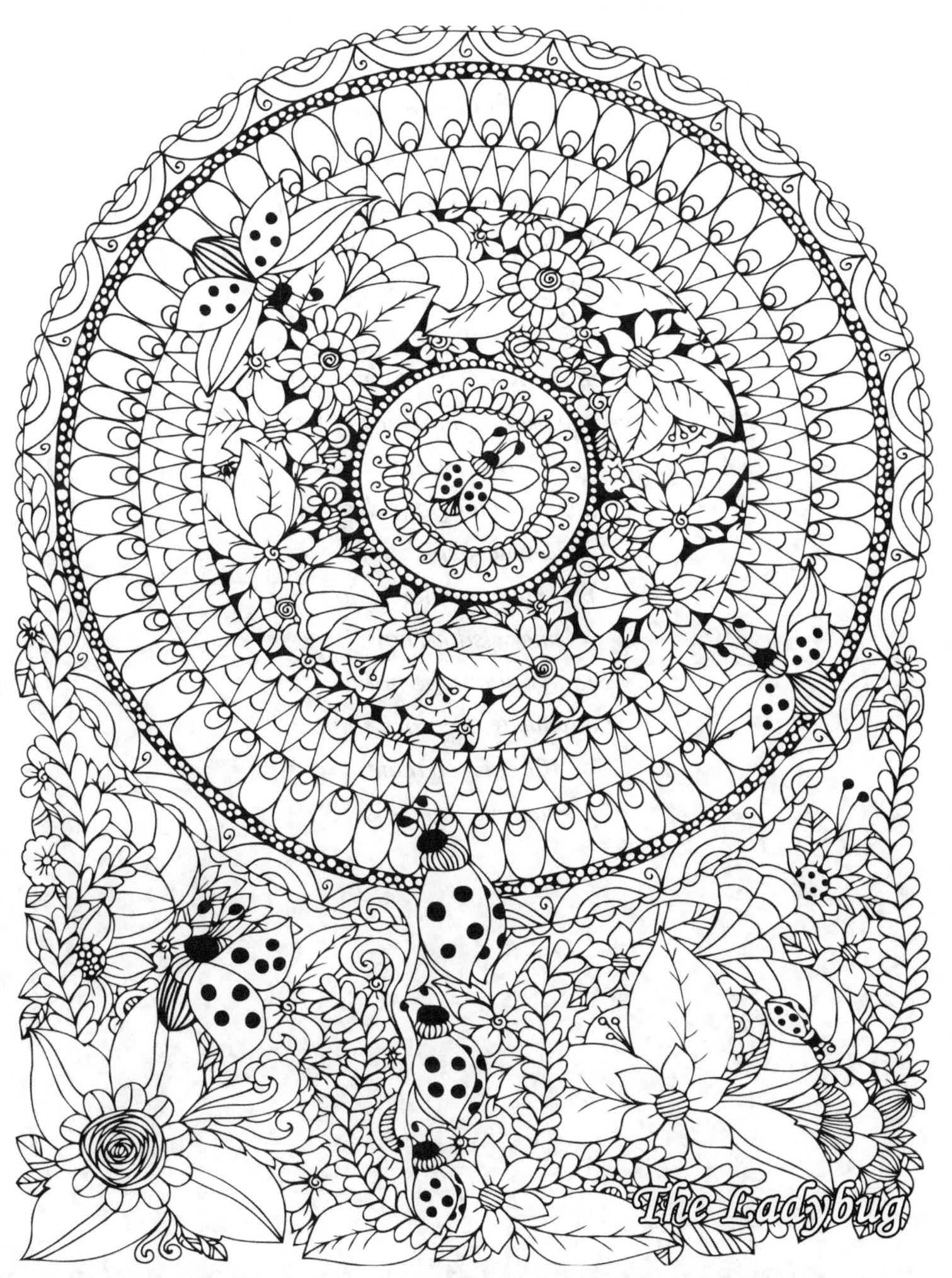

The Ladybug

Peacock

Air animals are amazing
messengers from the afterworld.
Their appearance is like
a sparkling diamond
from a loved one.
When the Peacock is your sign,
the message from your beloved
is a wonderful one...
"Acknowledge your dreams
and your aspirations.
You have greater vision
and wisdom now.
Stand out and be noticed.
Let your true colors shine.
If I can see them,
so can everyone else."

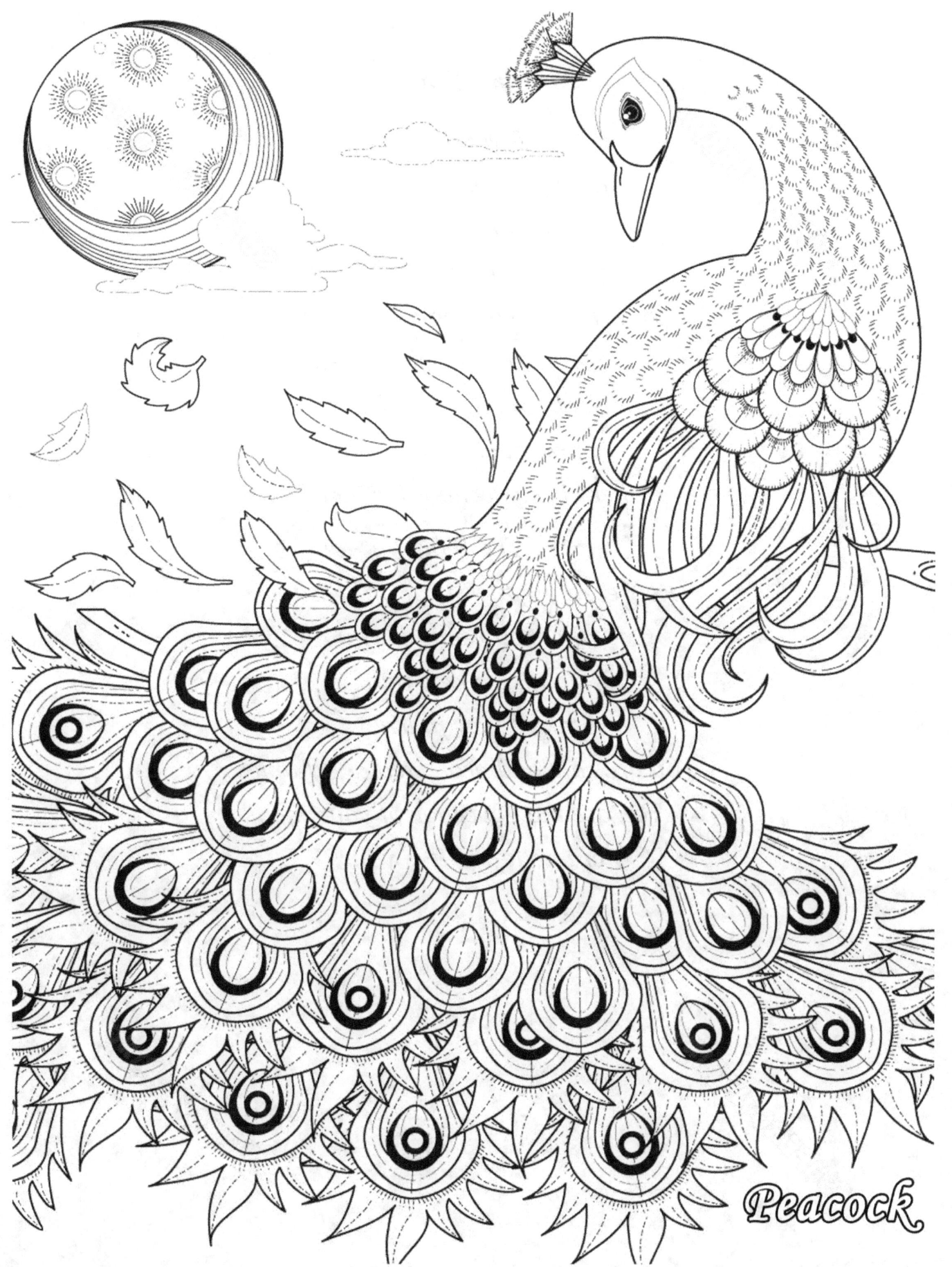

Peacock

The Wolf

When loved ones place
Animal Totems in our path,
they're not only letting us know
they're with us,
they are also giving us a uniquely
choreographed message...
"Love is in the air and to show you
how much I love you,
here is my symbol for you."

The Wolf:
Representing the Spirit of Freedom,
the wolf reminds you
to take a new path,
take a new journey.
You are safe and protected at all times.
You are the governor of your life;
create it and it is yours.

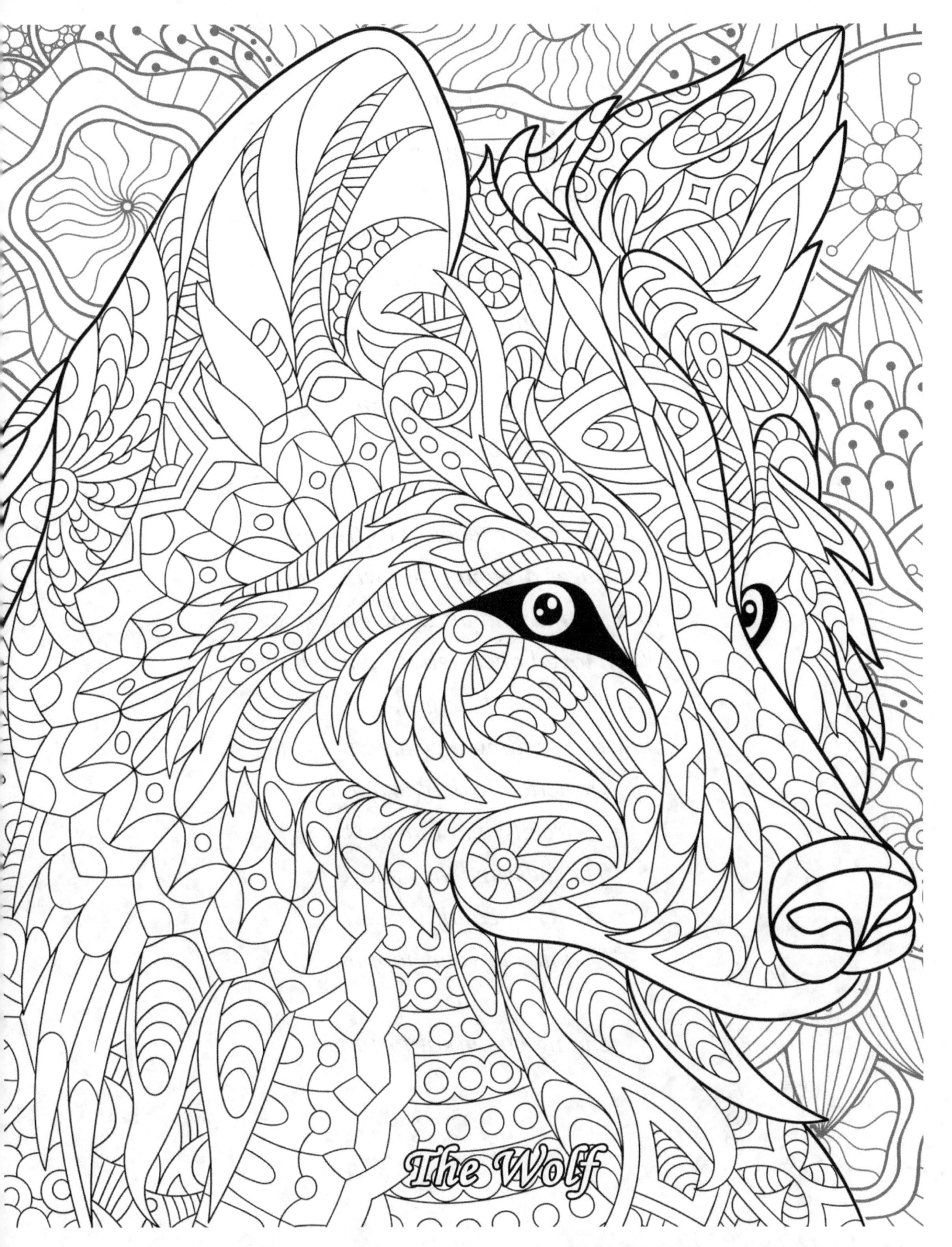

The Wolf

Rainbow

One of the many direct
paintings Nature creates
for us is the beautiful rainbow.
They are a powerful
sign from Spirit.
One that gently reminds us
to stay on our path,
don't be in a rush,
and don't get distracted.
The rainbow teaches us that its
treasures are ours that will come
in beautiful and unexpected forms.
When loved ones deliver a rainbow
as their gift,
they are sending a cosmic present,
practically delivering it
directly into our laps.
The message they share is
a very beautiful one...
"I rejoice in your happiness.
I'm here,
sending you great fortune."

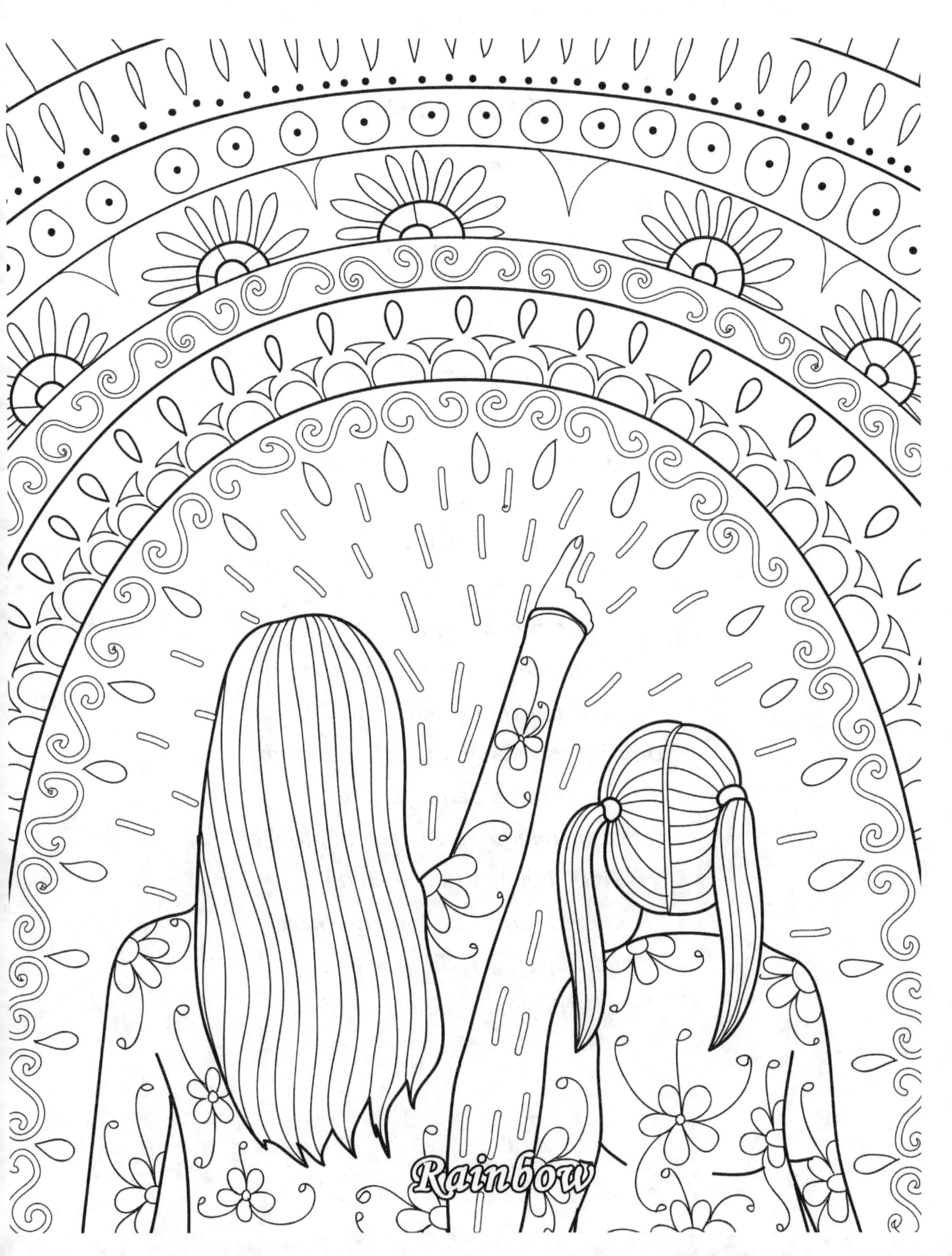

Rainbow

The Dragonfly

The dragonfly symbolizes transformation.
This amazing creature can appear
and disappear
in the blink of an eye.
It can shift colors
and race through time
and portals into other worlds.
A very powerful messenger,
the dragonfly is full
of mysticism,
magic,
and powers of illusion.
Like the butterfly, the message
your loved one shares when
you witness a dragonfly as your sign,
is quite beautiful…
"Yes, I'm right here. Please talk to me.
Tell me how you are feeling.
Pretend I haven't gone anywhere
and share everything with me.
I can hear you. I'm here to help."

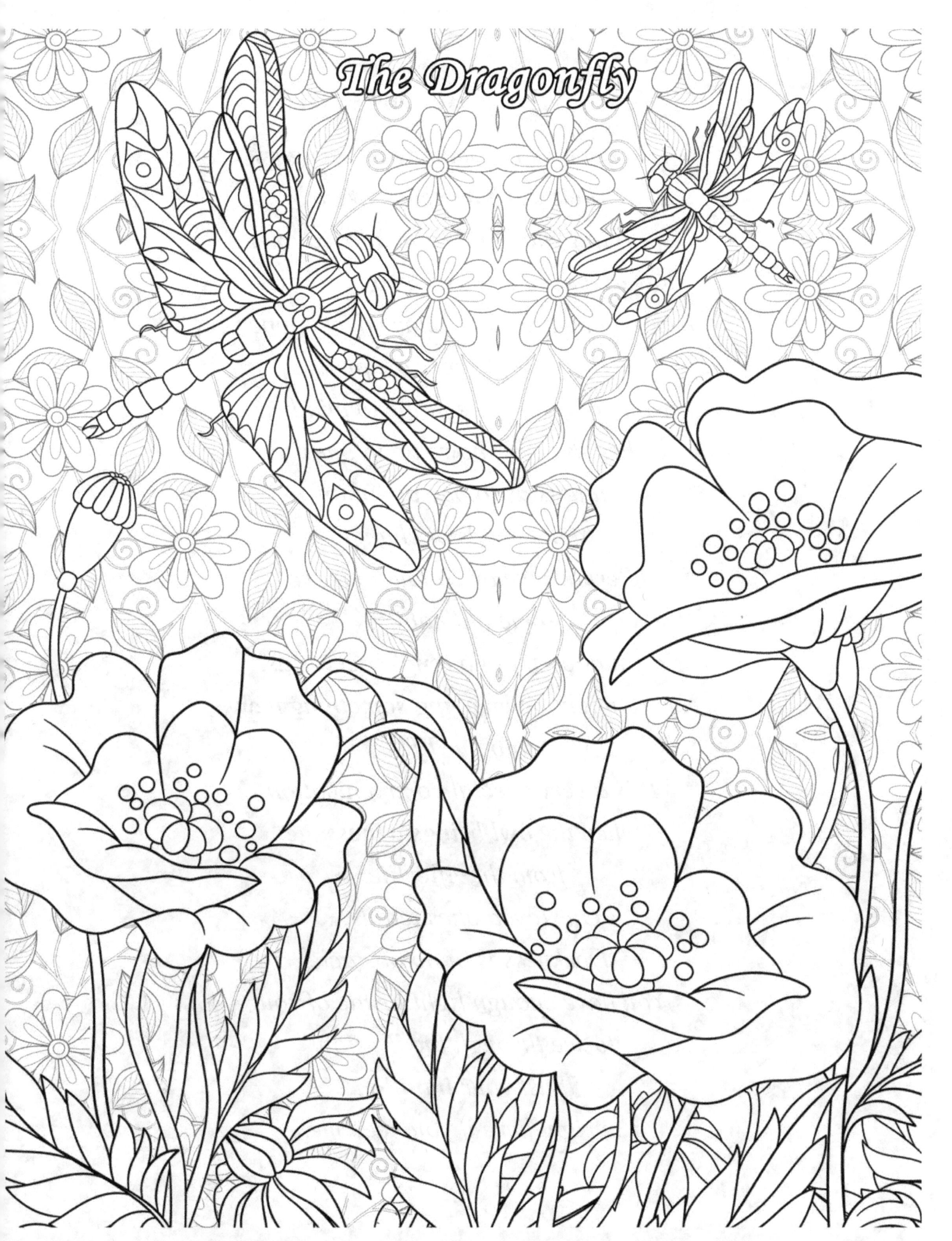

The Dragonfly

The Wise Owl

Air animals are amazing messengers.
Their appearance is like a
sparkling diamond from a loved one.
Revered as prophets, the owl can see,
feel, and hear events before they happen.
They are the seer of spirits
who pass from one plane to another.
When the owl shows up in our life,
it tells us to pay attention
to the winds of change.
Perhaps we are about to leave
some old habits,
a situation that no longer serves us,
or we might be bringing something new
into our life.
It is a very special communication
when the owl brings a message
from the Afterlife.
Our loved ones tell us...
"Darkness is of no obstacle.
You have enough light inside of you
to see through the illusion.
Trust your intuition.
I'm right here if you need me."

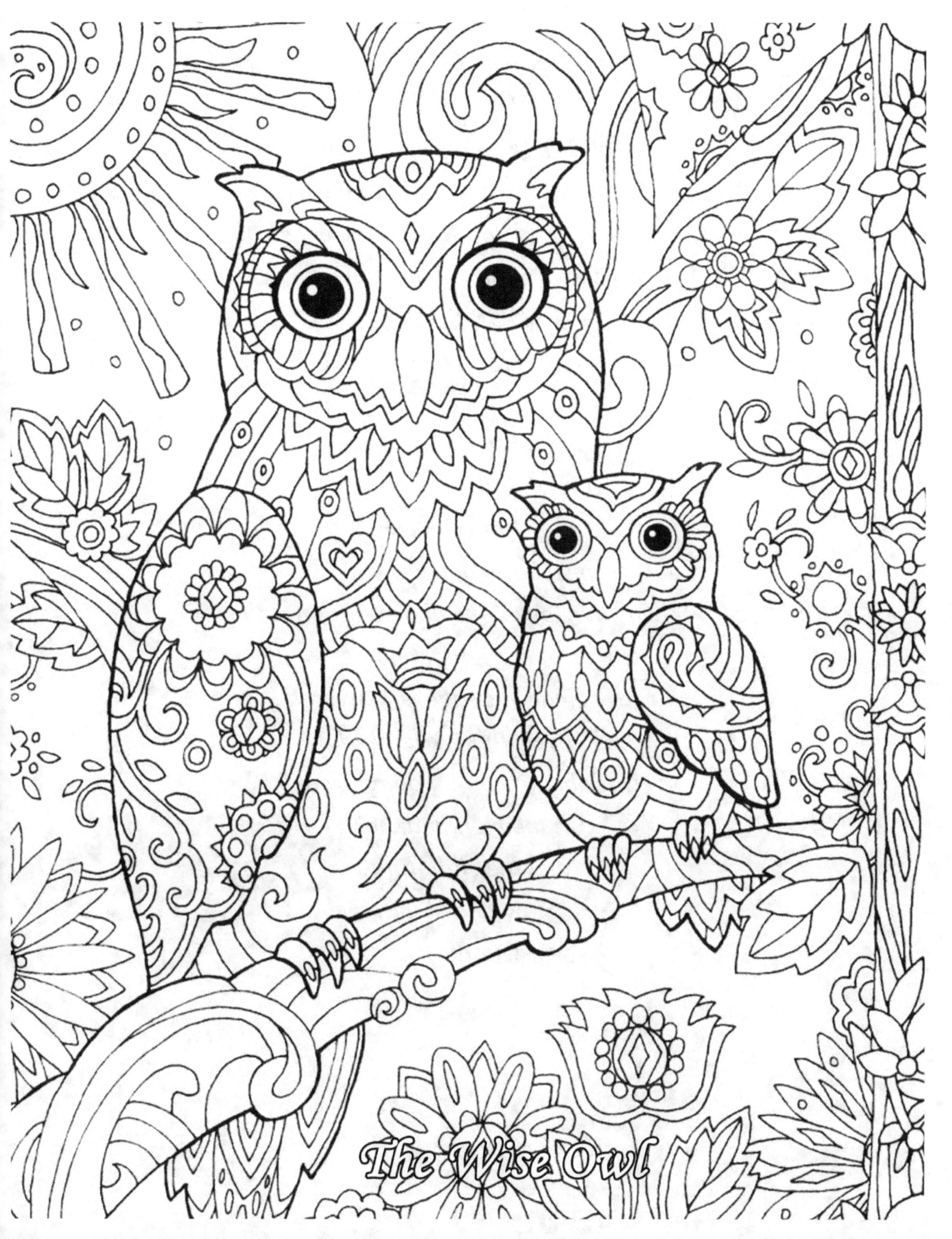

The Wise Owl

The Turtle

The Turtle is a grand symbol
for Mother Earth and Longevity.
They remind you to get connected
with your primal essence—
YOUR SOUL.
They tell you to recognize
the abundance before you
and to take your time,
allowing the flow of life
to work for you
instead of against you.
When your loved one chooses the Turtle
as their sign of choice,
a very clear message is delivered...
"Everything you need
is available to you if you approach it
in the right manner
and the right time.
Slow and steady
will win the race."

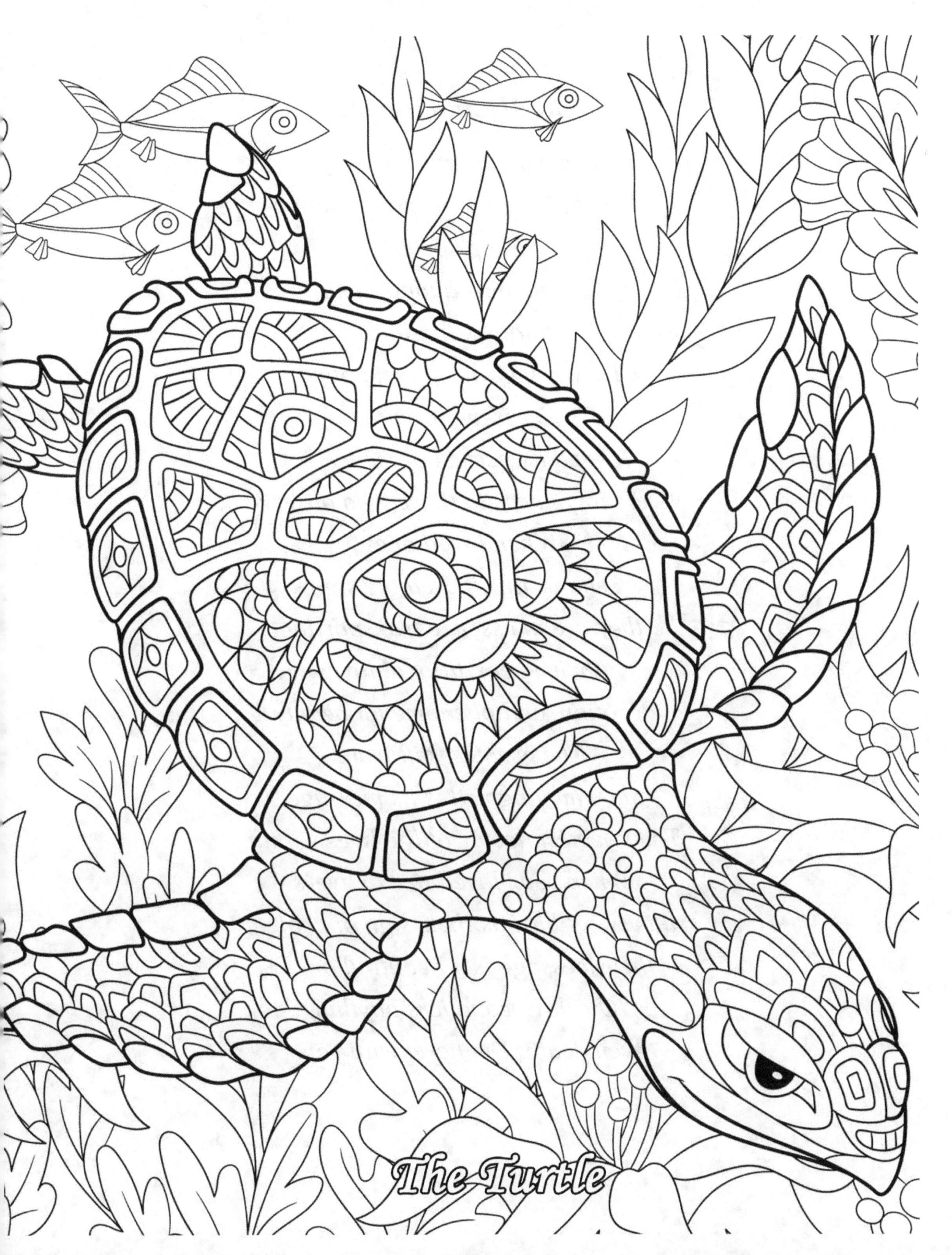

The Turtle

The Hummingbird

The only creature to stop

dead in its tracks while traveling

at top speed,

this tiny bird adapts easily

to any situation.

They bring love like no other

messenger can,

and its perfect presence

delivers joyfulness to those who observe it.

When loved ones

send us this incredible sign,

they are in essence transporting

their unconditional love,

devotion, and phenomenal beauty.

The greatest gift from

the hummingbird is its message:

The sweetest nectar of life lives within.

When your loved one delivers

this sweet bird as their sign of choice,

their message is a beautiful one...

"Our love conquers anything;

even death. I'm here, with you."

The Hummingbird

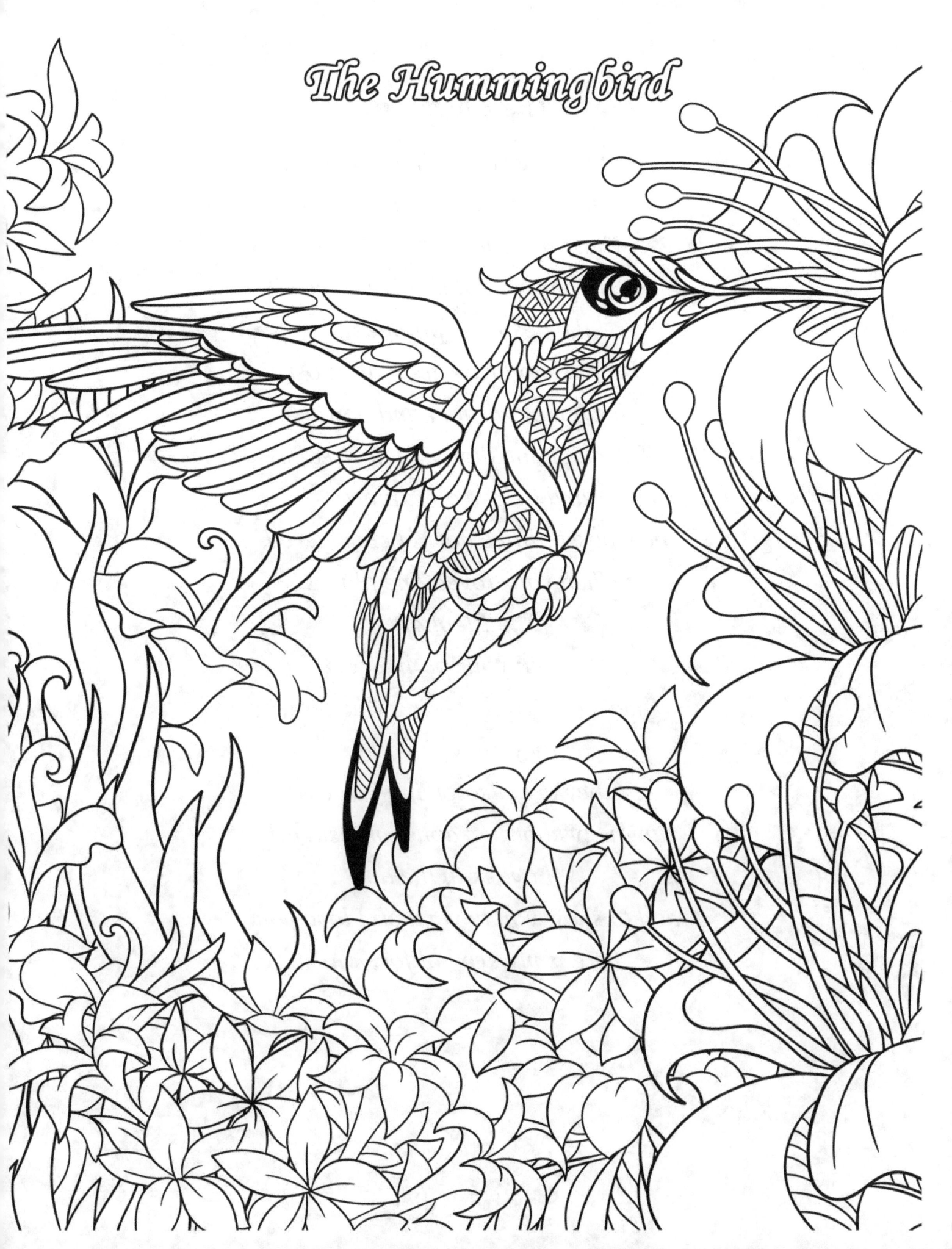

The Elephant

Embodying strength and power,
the elephant reminds you
what your life's driving force
is about and then gives you
the desire to pursue it.
Prepare to draw upon the most
ancient of wisdom and power.
The elephant shares their dreams
and helps you explore
new possibilities not yet considered.
When your loved one places
The Elephant
in your path,
they're not only letting you know
they're with you,
they are also giving you a
uniquely choreographed message…
"Love is in the air
and to show you how much I love you,
here is my symbol for you."

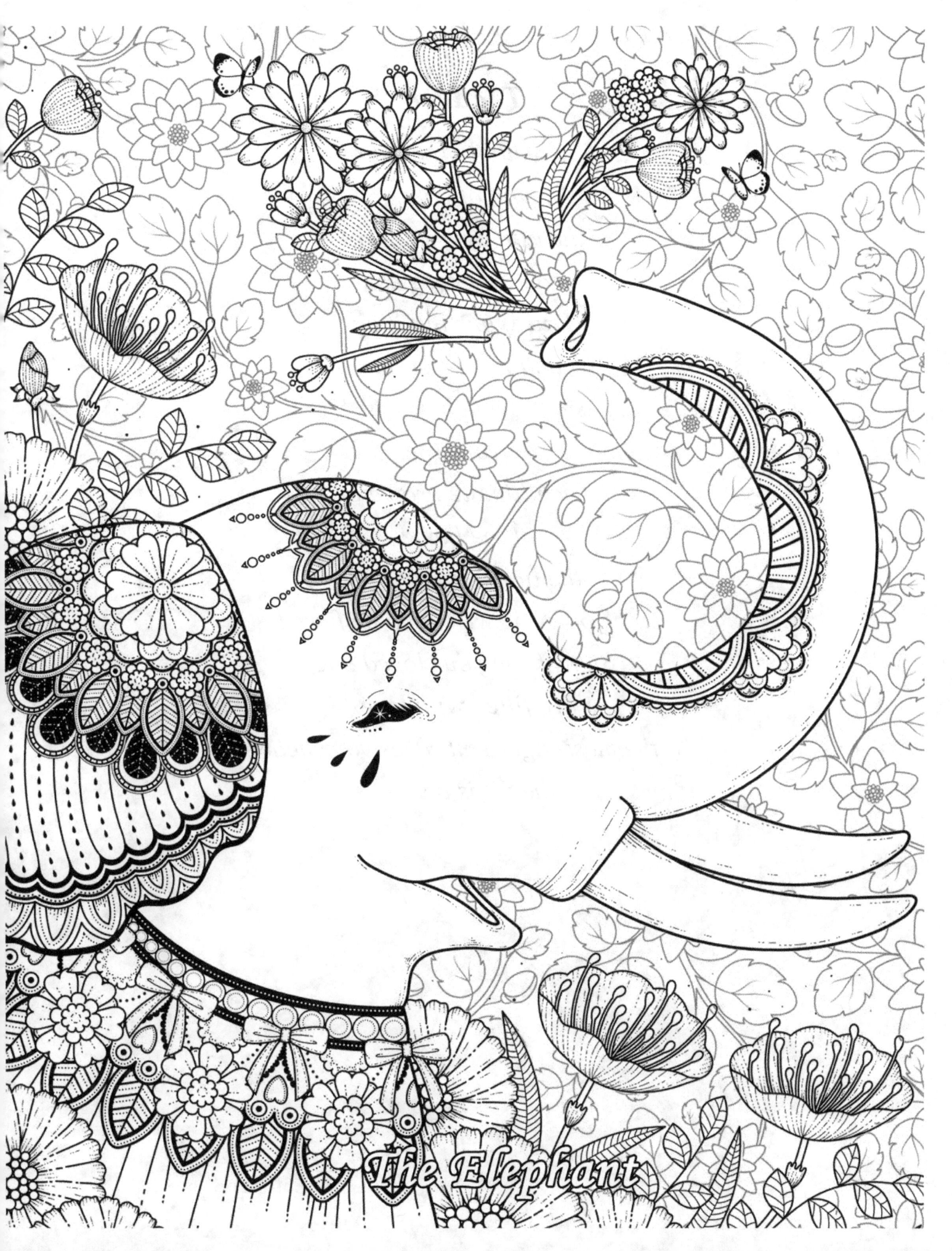

The Elephant

The Lion

A symbol of the sun
and of gold,
the lion awakens you
to new energies.
Trust your intuition
and imagination.
These will add new sunshine
to your life.
The ultimate protector
of the home,
the lion reminds you
to be bold, be wise, and be fierce.
Signs from your loved one
are filled with love.
If the messenger embraces your heart,
then it is a sign.

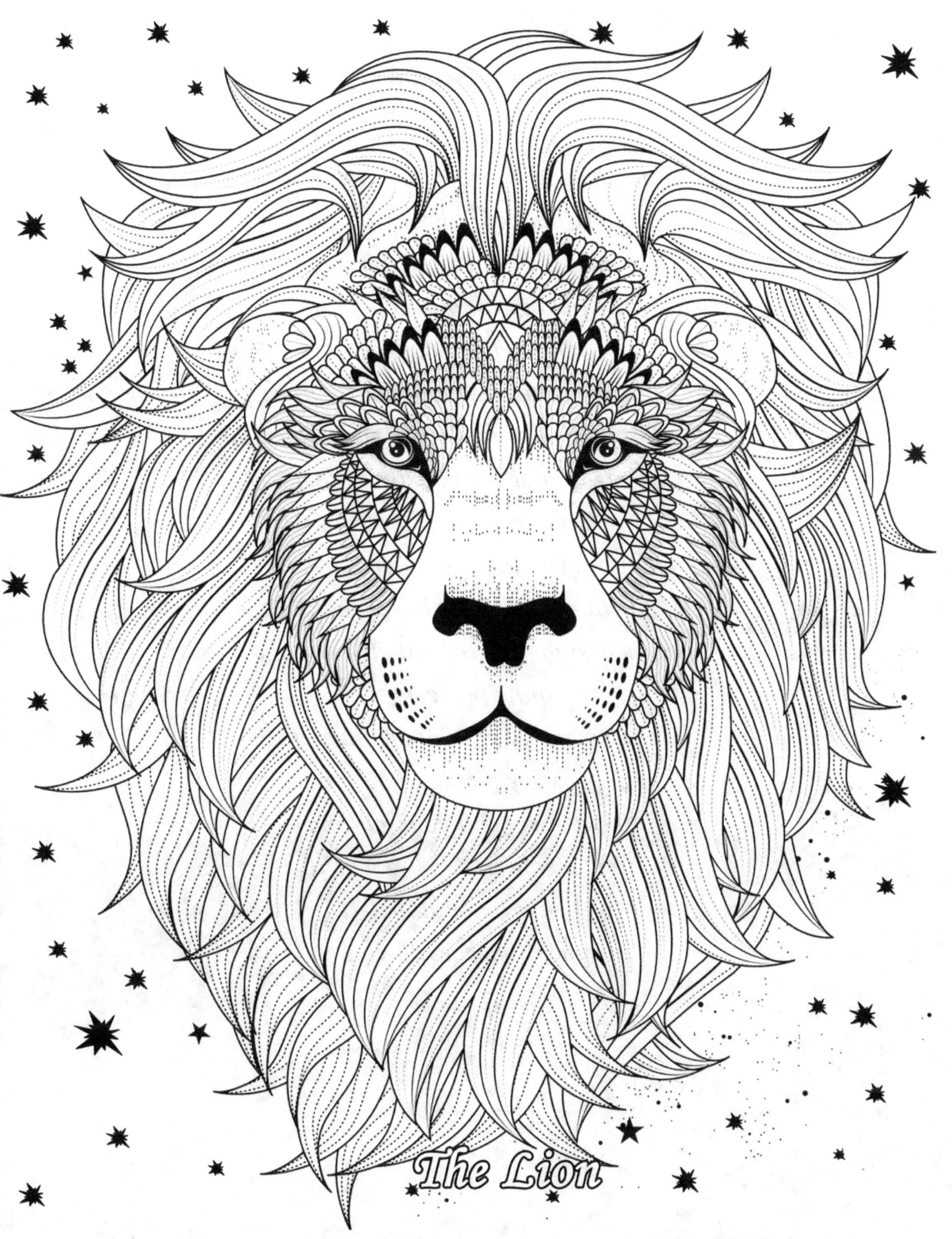

The Lion

The Panda

The wisdom of the panda
teaches us to move through life
calmly and with determination.
The panda is a powerful spirit animal
inspiring tranquil strength
and determination.
Under its soft and fuzzy appearance,
the Panda brings forth the importance of
strong personal boundaries to feel safe
and grounded in life.
The panda is a symbol of gentleness and strength.
When your loved one shares the Panda
as their sign of choice, their message
is quite powerful…
"Remember the importance of
establishing your personal boundaries to
be at ease with yourself and
to feel safe in this big world.
You are not alone—
I'm right here with you."

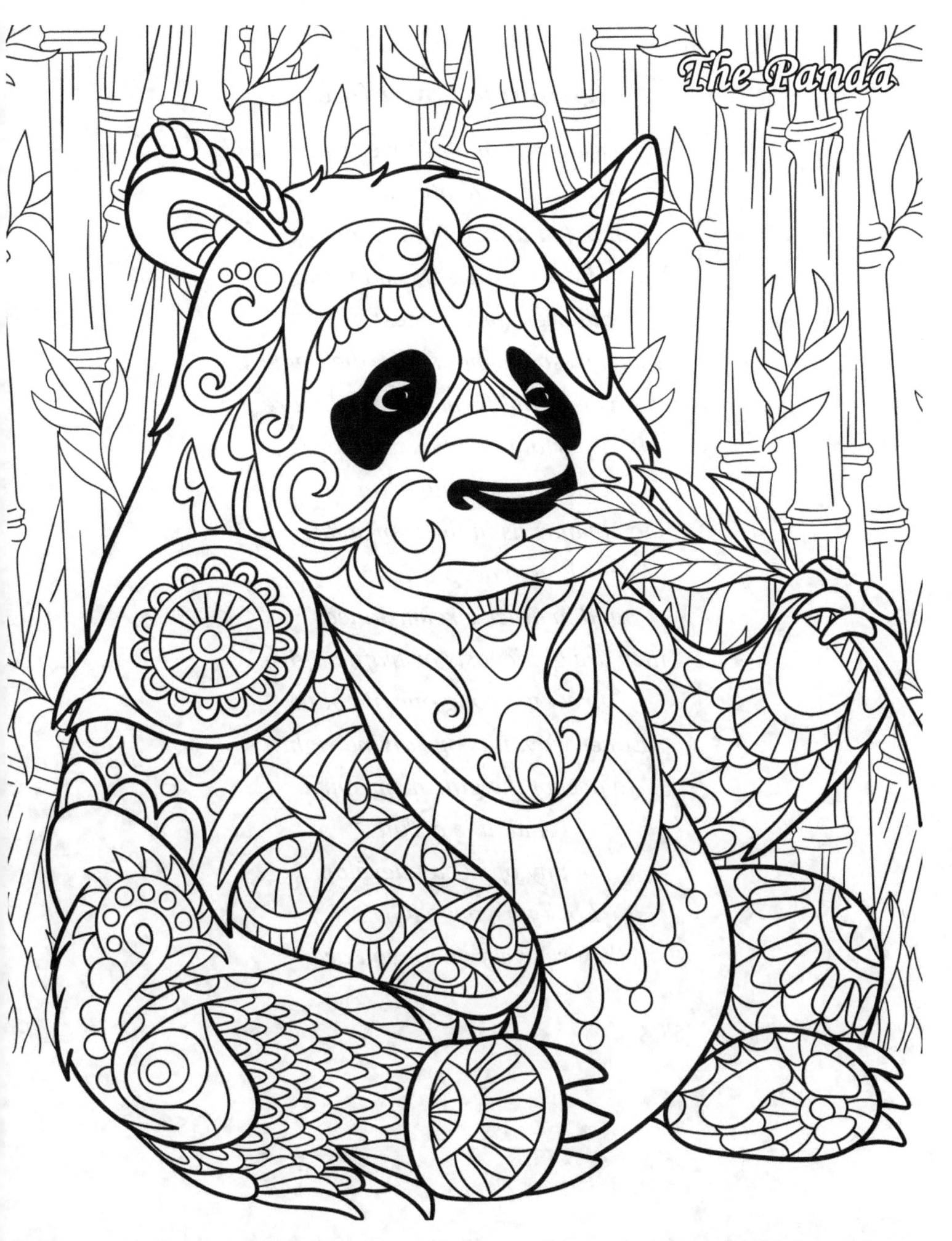

The Panda

Signs From Loved Ones

Messages from our loved ones,
when identified,
can potentially be life changing.
Most often, they are the subtle signs,
but even the slightest ones
are the messages that speak the loudest.
Any sign or signal from the spiritual realm
is important and has a purpose.
Sometimes the signs appear
to comfort us in times of sadness
and deep grief
and in other circumstances,
they are guideposts or traffic lights
to direct us along our life path.
Either way, it is our divine right
to accept the gifts from spirit.
And, it is a skill
that any of us can develop.
Look for your SIGNS...
they're everywhere you are.

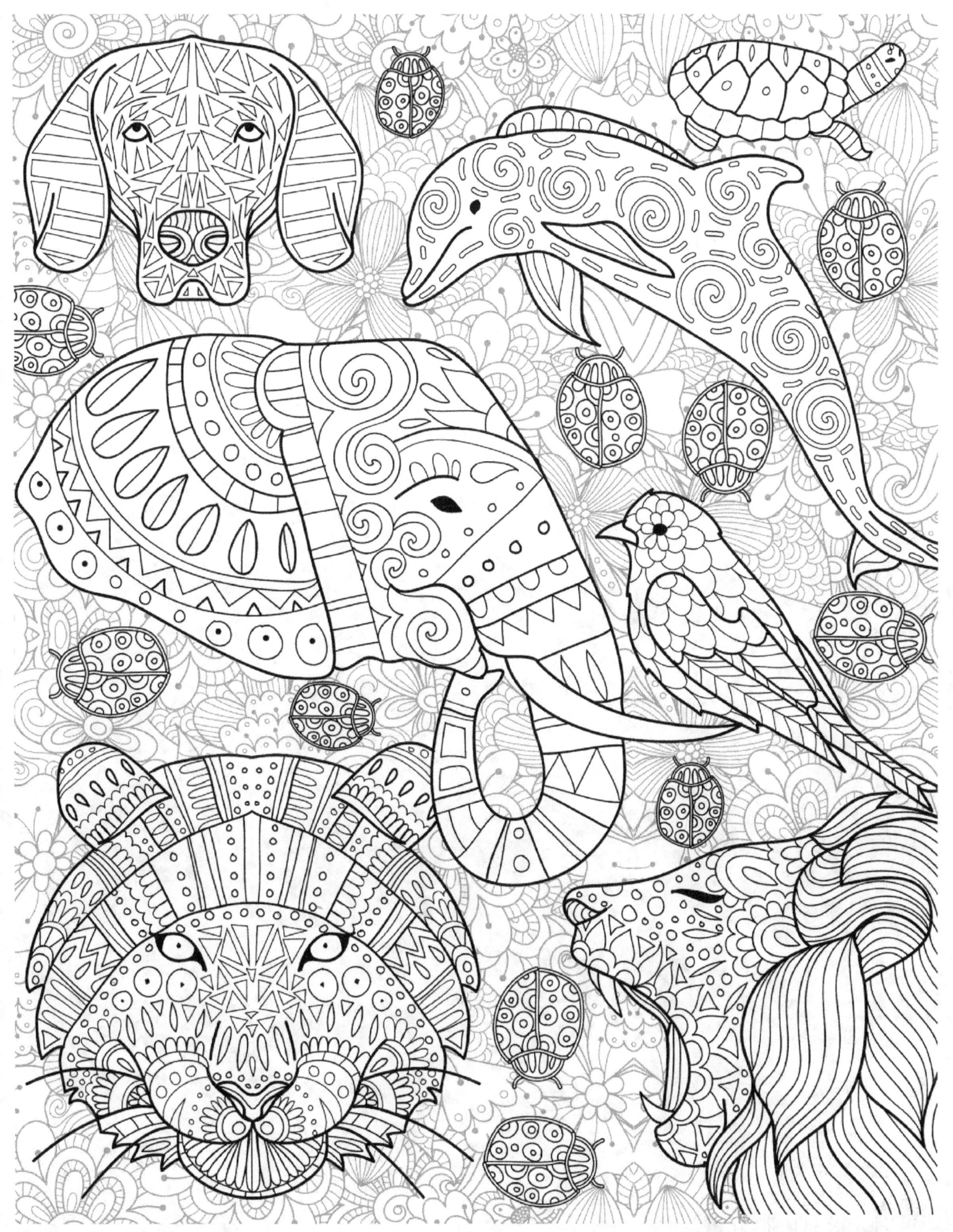